AIRFIX
magazine guide 19

Model Soldiers

Martin Windrow and Gerry Embleton

Patrick Stephens Ltd
in association with Airfix Products Ltd

First published — 1976

ISBN 0 85059 234 8

Don't forget these other Airfix Magazine Guides!

No 1 *Plastic Modelling*
by Gerald Scarborough
No 3 *Military Modelling*
by Gerald Scarborough
No 4 *Napoleonic Wargaming*
by Bruce Quarrie
No 5 *Tank & AFV Modelling*
by Gerald Scarborough
No 8 *German Tanks of World War 2*
by Terry Gander and
Peter Chamberlain
No 9 *Ancient Wargaming*
by Phil Barker
No 12 *Afrika Korps*
by Bruce Quarrie
No 13 *The French Foreign Legion*
by Martin Windrow
No 15 *World War 2 Wargaming*
by Bruce Quarrie
No 17 *British Tanks of World War 2*
by Terry Gander and
Peter Chamberlain
No 20 *8th Army in the Desert*
by John Sandars
(Full list available on request)

Cover design by Tim McPhee

Text set in 8 on 9pt Univers Medium
by David Green (Printers) Limited,
Kettering, Northants.
Printed on Fineblade cartridge 90 gsm
and bound by the Garden City Press,
Letchworth, Herts.
Published by Patrick Stephens
Limited, Bar Hill, Cambridge, CB3 8EL,
in association with Airfix Products
Limited, London SW18.

Contents

Editor's introduction

The purpose of this book is to introduce younger and less experienced modellers to the possibilities of military figure modelling with 54mm plastic kits; and to suggest conversion ideas to modellers who have got to grips with the hobby but who have not yet progressed far beyond making up the kits exactly according to the instructions. There may even be one or two ideas in the later chapters which are of interest to experienced veterans; but basically this book is intended as a primer.

This does *not* mean that the authors in any way 'talk down' to the younger modeller, or discourage him from taking risks—far from it. The steady improvement in the standard and finish of one's models is the great pleasure of this hobby. With increasing practice comes increasing skill, and with skill comes the confidence to tackle projects which would have scared the modeller away not long before. The great reward is to realise that it is becoming easier, and more certain, to recreate on the modelling table the image in the mind which fired the imagination.

The subjects selected for the conversions range in period over several centuries, but naturally most of the space has been devoted to periods which are particularly popular with modellers, especially the Napoleonic Wars and World War 2. In most cases the authors have taken as their basis the kits in the Airfix 54mm range, as being inexpensive and easily available. With the appearance in 1975 of the 8th Army and Afrika Korps Multipose sets, splendid new opportunities were opened up for the converter. The authors have allowed themselves the luxury of one or two rather exotic subjects, both for their own enjoyment and to encourage modellers to allow their imaginations to range widely as they study the contents of their kits and spares trays. In a few cases, simply because they illustrate particular points or areas of subject they wished to touch upon, the authors have used illustrations and subjects which have already appeared in the course of their two series of articles in *Airfix Magazine*; I hope readers who have already seen them will forgive this logical short-cut, and that there are enough new ideas in the book to pacify them.

While the authors have tried to give brief notes on painting and colour schemes with most conversions, I must stress that this book is mainly about *modelling*. In the appropriate places will be found lists of recommended reference sources for colour schemes, but if the authors had tried to go into great detail on each conversion the number of models covered would have been much smaller, and I do not think this would have been any great service to our readers.

BRUCE QUARRIE

one

Clearing for action

The modelling bench

The first requirement for this, as for every other branch of modelling is somewhere to work. If you are coming into figure modelling from some other area of the hobby like aircraft or AFV modelling, we presume you already have the basic necessities. For those who are beginners in the whole field, the following remarks may be helpful.

The first model the author ever made—on the top of a chest of drawers, standing up—was a 1:48 scale Aurora Spitfire. It was several centuries ago, when the author was about 11 years old, that this incident occurred. He built the kit, which had about seven parts, in an hour flat. Being impatient to see the finished result, he did not wait for the cement to dry before starting the next step, and as a result the comparative angles of wings, tailplane, etc, presented an interesting picture of random variety. Not realising that cement should be applied sparingly, with a pin or cocktail-stick, he squeezed it straight from the nozzle of the tube on to the required spot, so every joint had a thick, uneven collar of excess cement round it. As the hour wore on, the excess round the nozzle built up and blocked the tube. Rather than sticking a pin through this, or cleaning the nozzle, the author merely squeezed harder. This squirted several pence' worth of cement out in a flood over some joints, softening the wing-roots like tarmac on a hot day. Having no paints of the correct shade, he painted the spinner and, as an afterthought, the rudder with a gloss house-paint of a startling crimson, which melted the surface of the plastic. Transfers proved something of a disaster, as some stuck in the wrong places and others broke up in the water and were lost for good. All in all, the result was a text-book example of what *not* to do. It is usually said that we must all learn from our own mistakes, and cannot be warned by those of others. It is the author's sincere hope that readers will learn from *his*. Why be an idiot yourself, when you can watch a genuine one at work?

If you have a room of your own you have no problem; if not you will have to try to establish your modelling empire firmly in some convenient corner, with at least a table or working surface from which all hazards such as dusting mothers are warned off by threat of savage reprisals. The great thing is to be able to leave a model half built, in the middle of an orderly chaos which *you* understand even if no one else does, in the confident knowledge that it will be untouched when you return to it. If you haven't got a table, then make a modelling tray which you can carry around; a big sheet of rigid hardboard or laminate makes a good one, with a raised edge for preference, and the smooth side upwards. When you set yourself up for work, make sure the relative height of chair and work-top allow you to work at a comfortable angle—concentration will disguise the lumbar agonies you are inviting until you straighten up, to find yourself crippled! Another absolute essential is a good light, preferably an anglepoise or similar desk lamp which you can direct to make a pool of bright light on your work surface without shining into your eyes. This cannot be stressed too much—you can't make delicate models in this scale by feel! An ordinary overhead room light is no good at all, and will have as evil effects on your eyesight as on your model. If working by daylight, try to set up your bench in a window, or near one, where direct sunshine falls. If you have a permanent working area, then keep your various tools and accessories in special places—paints in one box, knives and files in another, plastic card and scrap sprue in another—so that you can find what you need in a hurry. Old kit boxes are useful here, especially for things like bottled liquid cement, turps, and so forth. There can be few more harrowing experiences than knocking over a bottle of turps with a careless elbow and seeing it flood over a virtually finished model, ruining evenings of painstaking work. Do it once, and forever afterwards you will be pathologically careful to rack bottles where they cannot fall over. A large scrap paper pad, for smears of paint and cement, is also an essential for clean work.

Tools

Assuming you are a beginner, for pity's sake don't be so eager to produce something that you start with inadequate tools. A pen-knife and a tube of cement simply will not do! For a very modest price you can kit yourself up like a veteran, and it is always worth the expense and effort to do so. Modellers of many years' standing have usually acquired a weird and wonderful set of tools, gadgets and implements, sometimes including quite expensive machinery like miniature welding tools, electric drills, spray guns, vices, clamps, and sets of scalpels that would do Jack the Ripper credit. You can make models of a highly professional standard without all this gear, although it is very comforting to have it eventually.

Simple conversion from Airfix Rifleman into US 'Greyjacket' of the war of 1812, as described in Airfix Magazine, *November 1975. The addition of a knee-patch gives individual character to an otherwise rather featureless uniform. The scenic base, made very simply with a wooden spill 'fence' and a bit of grass matting, together with the choice of animation—a pause for a 'wet' during wood-chopping for the squad cooking fire—add a lot to the appeal of the model, for little extra effort. Always be open to ideas for posing your model in a really lifelike and individual way.*

Study old military paintings and prints for conversion ideas. Those of the late 19th and early 20th Century usually have a lot of strong animation and flamboyant feeling. This scene of a Frenchman being searched by Prussians during the Franco-Prussian War provides ideas for at least three 'mini-dioramas' which would work well in 54mm scale. The lolling officers with their laden lunch table are a natural for a model. The prisoner-being-searched theme is an idea full of possibilities for super-detailing and can be set in any period of history. The orderly, with his covered basket with protruding bottles, could be posed with the inn maid in a simple but pleasing duo. With Airfix Napoleonic and World War 2 figure kits, and one or two of the inexpensive Almark books on Imperial German cavalry units and the Franco-Prussian War for reference, all these ideas could be pursued by modellers of average skill.

The first essential is a razor-sharp modelling knife. We recommend one of the cheaper makes which consists of a hard plastic handle into which you can slip the various blades. You are going to use a lot of blades, so get into the habit of buying in bulk; you can ruin good work with a blunt blade, so don't hesitate to ditch one as soon as it looses its keeness. For a pound you can buy a handle and several blades. Some experts swear by exotically shaped blades; in practice we believe that there are few jobs you cannot tackle with one straight-edged blade with a sharp point, and one rounded-edge blade. Stock up on these blades, half-a-dozen at a time; they cost a matter of pence, and are a good investment. *Handle them with respect at all times*; they are deadly weapons, and can open a vein or cut down to the bone if you treat them carelessly. *Never* cut at an angle which puts a sideways stress on a blade. They are thin, and break easily and suddenly, sometimes with gory results. *Never* cut towards your fingers, at an angle which will push the blade into your irreplaceable carcass if it slips over the point of pressure and continues in a straight line. Like a gun, a modelling knife is neutral; whether it works for good or ill depends entirely on the moron holding it.

After a knife, your next requirement is a selection of fine modelling files. In recent years these have become more readily available, and are much less expensive than they once were. They are known as 'Swiss files', and most good model shops and craft shops stock them. If you are living in an area badly served by the trade, then check the classified and small advertisements in modelling magazines such as *Airfix Magazine, Military Modelling, Scale Models,* and so on; you will find mail-order offers most months. Swiss files are usually sold in sets of five or six, for between one and two pounds the set. If you are buying them individually over the counter, you can confidently limit yourself to three basic shapes. You will find endless uses for a thin, round-section 'rat-tail' file; a triangular-section file tapering to a sharp point, with three flat surfaces; and a file with one half-round face and one flat one. Again, they will cost you less than a pound for the lot, and are well worth it: as is the trouble of getting a good pair of stainless steel surgical tweezers from the chemist.

A razor-saw is the next requirement, for those cuts through thick objects which are difficult and tedious to make with a knife, and impossible to make cleanly. There are various proprietary brands available, so shop around. Get the thinnest blade you can find; we find that made by X-acto very satisfactory, but there are others as good.

A sharp, fine point of hard steel is

always useful for boring. Most modellers have some old tool or gadget which they swear by, and which started life as something else entirely. We have a much-prized 'hand-spike' in the form of one half of an old pair of brass compasses with a long steel point. You could do worse than hunt up one of these. Also, keep a supply of pins on

The actual appearance of the soldier on campaign differs sharply from the uniform regulations — this sketch of one of Napoleon's infantrymen on the march gives an idea for a conversion of the Airfix French Line Infantry 1815 kit, with bits from the Imperial Guard Grenadier, such as long trousers and epaulettes. The coat is the main challenge, but with ingenuity and either modelling putty or plastic-impregnated paper it could be made from the Airfix Foreign Legionnaire kit. Historex spares offer a delightfully detailed sprue of cauldron, pots and pans; and the firewood bundle can be made from tiny twig-ends.

8

the work-bench. These days—and not before time—shirt manufacturers are starting to use pins with big round plastic heads for fastening new shirts in their packages; these are easier to handle than the old kind, and less painful to push into things. Keep a bundle of cocktail-sticks handy, as well, for a hundred and one chores on the modelling table; and a steel ruler.

Cements

Tube polystyrene cement is the usual adhesive for modelling, and is available in a dozen brands. All are more or less identical. Keep a couple of tubes handy at all times. Remember to use it very sparingly, applying it to the often-tiny surfaces of model components with the point of a pin or cocktail-stick. There seems to be no rule about the quality of cement; some tubes of one given brand will be fine, others of the same brand will dry too fast, clog, and string. Wait till the second you need it, squeeze a small pool on to your scrap paper, dip up a little on your pin, and use it. Never return to the same pool of cement more than ten seconds or so after squeezing it out, as it will already have started to skin over, thicken and string. This is an expensive way of using cement, and one of the reasons why we strongly recommend the use of a liquid cement. There are several main brands; Humbrol make a good one. Its advantages are numerous. Using a fine-pointed paintbrush, you can take out exactly as much as you need without wasting any. You can apply it much more cleanly and with greater control to fine pieces of plastic. There should be no excess at all, and even if minute amounts spill out of a joint they will dry flat and invisible. Working slowly and carefully, you can produce a model of infinitely better finish than would be possible with tube cement; and once you get the hang of it, liquid cement is much more versatile. Long live liquid cement, and all who sail in her! But our comment on guarding against knocking over bottles of turps applies with double force to liquid cement. Not a week before writing these lines we reached for a pair of tweezers without looking, and spilled a full bottle over a model which was in the last stages of a tricky conversion. Eyes starting, we watched the work of hours literally dissolving on the bench . . . You can't take too many experiences like that without becoming permanently embittered, so treat your bottled cement with care.

Putty

An essential for the converter is a tube of modelling filler, or 'body putty'. Hereafter, please note that this is the stuff we mean when we mention 'putty'—not the goop you fix window-panes with. There are, again, several brands. Humbrol do one, and so do Squadron, an American firm, whose imported 'Green Stuff' is highly regarded by most modellers. If your local shop doesn't stock it, check the magazine small-ads again—it is available in this country by mail. Use it according to the manufacturer's instructions; and it isn't a bad idea to allow even longer for drying than they recommend. Its consistency is delightful, and easy to work when tacky with a tool dipped in water to prevent tagging. When dry it can be cut or filed. A new epoxy putty, which you mix from two compounds, has also earned glowing reports—we haven't tried it ourselves yet but it sounds excellent. The trade name is 'Milliput' and it costs 45p from 78 Mount Drive, Manchester N31 1QA.

Plastic card

Various grades and thicknesses of polystyrene card, usually in sheets about eight inches by ten, are widely available. One sheet of each of about four normal grades should last you for a long time. Note, also, that in Airfix figure kits you are given a generous little sheet of very thin card, for belts and strapping. Always keep the unused portions of this most useful material. Slice it with your modelling knife, using your steel ruler to keep a straight line.

'Plastic soup'

This is the one thing you can't buy over the counter, but it is very easy to

Spirited Job drawing of French troops in Egypt during the Pyramids campaign. This sort of thing is a goldmine for the ambitious modeller, who can modify and paint to his heart's content, and turn the basic kit figures of any period into a completely new and dazzling group, by careful selection of reference and imaginative animation (National Army Museum).

make. The idea is to have at all times a jar of liquid polystyrene, about the consistency of thin honey, which you can paint or blob on to modelling work with an old paintbrush. It dries reasonably quickly, and makes a perfect painting surface. It has many uses, which practice will teach you. It can be used, in slowly built-up layers, to fill cracks and depressions and hide join-lines. It can be painted over putty additions, so that the material of the model will have a uniform painting surface. It can be painted over pieces of paper when you are doing conversions which involve, for instance, adding new tunic skirts. It can be used with great control, to build up hair and beards, thicken limbs, mend breaks, and generally hide a thousand sins. Throughout the rest of this book it will be referred to simply as 'soup'.

To make 'soup', buy a jar of Windsor and Newton 'Winsol' paint remover and solvent from an artists' supplies shop. Pour off half into another jar; both jars should have tightly fitting

screw lids. Now chop up a load of polystyrene sprue from old kits, or polystyrene card, into small pieces, and drop them into the jars of 'Winsol'. Pile them in for a bit, then stir the stew with a cocktail stick, then close the lid and shake hard for a few minutes, then start all over again. Keep going until the scrap is completely dissolved, then add more and start again. This process will take several hours, but still you can do it in intervals of another job. It's best to leave it overnight to see how saturated the solution is. The object is to go on until no more plastic will dissolve, and the jars contain a thick white goop the consistency of thin honey. Tightly closed, this will keep forever. When you need it, dip it out with an old paintbrush.

The spares box

Many experienced modellers take as much pride in a well-stocked spares box as in finished models, and with reason. It is the one vital sign of the serious modeller, the man who intends

10   Model Soldiers

Conversions need not always be complex to be attractive. This splendidly wooden studio portrait of a late Victorian British cavalry NCO gives an idea for a nice modification of the Airfix 95th Rifleman kit. With a minimum of work and 'props' a completely new character can be achieved.

to take this hobby on and lick it! The principle need hardly be spelled out: *never throw away any part of a model kit*. Optional parts of figures, tanks, aircraft, horses, trucks, ships, guns — throw them all in there. You may swear never to make another aircraft — but that aerial will make a bayonet scabbard one day, and that drop-tank has a domed end which may, in the fullness of time, reappear on the head of a Norman knight. It's not just the obviously valuable heads, hands, shakos, muskets and pouches that are worth keeping, it's *anything* — what it was originally moulded to represent is irrelevant beside its potential to become something quite different. It is surprising how quickly you can build up a good rich compost in the spares box, if you follow the golden rule. Even sprue should be kept — it can be rendered down into 'soup', or chopped

up and carved into 1,001 things; or even, if nothing more interesting occurs, used to stir paint! The art of 'stretching' it over a candle to make fine plastic filaments has been described many times elsewhere, and we won't take the space here; but stretched sprue is as useful to the figure modeller as in any other branch of the hobby.

Scenic bases

Many modellers are satisfied with producing single figures on their own bases; many others like to build up diorama scenes of varying size, from couples to quite large groups of figures with extensive landscape and props, even buildings. Whichever category you fall into, the art of making convincing scenic bases can transform the finished appearance of your model.

Certain basic principles apply, although there is no point in our giving a lot of space to detailed descriptions of individual layouts. One good rule is *restraint*. It takes time and practice to make convincing 'ground', 'grass', 'rocks', 'desert', and so on, and it is particularly difficult to make 'bushes' which look realistic. The usual materials are putty for the basic ground, with small gauge gravel (try aquarium gravel) or cork shavings, flock to roughen the surface, and odd bits of stone and twig. Sisal string, soaked until it loses its twist and cut into irregular lengths, can be pushed into soft putty to make very convincing long grass or cereal crops. Fine sand, preferably 'silver' sand from lawn dressings, can be patiently scattered over hardened putty ground painted with liquid adhesive. Paint your ground with soft, muted colours, dry-brushing one shade over others to make them blurred and indistinct. Look at the real thing, and note how few primary colours you see, and how many widely varying shades of subtle colour earth can take on depending on soil and weather. Nowadays you can get very pleasing sheets of grass 'matting' from shops stocking railway layout supplies; used sparingly this makes convincing lawns. We repeat, look at the real thing, and note the combinations and groups of natural materials and textures. In nature you don't find a lump of rough rock sitting by itself on top of a stretch of trimmed grass; you don't find bright green foliage in a desert landscape. Use your eyes—this is the one type of reference which the Almighty provides for free!

'Props'

Kits are usually designed to depict a soldier in a parade or combat position, with full equipment. The converter will wish to animate his models, to give them an individual character, to produce a model unique in conception and appearance. A lot can be done with the materials provided in the kit and a little imagination; if you build up a good stock of scale 'props', even more is possible. Cultivate the habit of seeing things with a '54mm scale eye'. There are some manufacturers, notably Rose and Historex, whose spare parts lists are a feast of jugs, bottles, artillery and pioneer tools, weapons, headgear, buckets, wheels, and so on. Phoenix make superb period furniture and fittings. Tamiya tank kits now contain splendid 'stowage' gear like odd boxes and crates and wash-bowls and tools. Careful hunts in toy shops may pay off with finely moulded farm and domestic animals of a suitable size for 'camp life' and 'foraging' dioramas. Keep your eyes open, and whether or not you have an immediate project in mind, bear these treasures home and put them in the spares box. One day you will find the perfect model for them.

References

The best modeller in the world is only as good as his references; without information, you are helpless. So cultivate the habit of grabbing reference wherever you see it. Never let a magazine or colour supplement get thrown in the garbage in your house without checking it first. There may be a colour photo of a painting with a military subject, or a reproduction of some old sepia photo of Imperial days in India. There may be a recruiting advertisement with a colour photo-graph of some grinning matelot or serious-looking armoured car commander. Perhaps it's just a photo of a racehorse—but when you first try painting a horse you'll be grateful for the help it gives in identifying light and shade. It may be only an after-shave advert; but if the colour photo of the male model's face is well lit, it may be invaluable when you come to painting your next model's face, in showing just how the shadow falls in an eye-socket. All this stuff is free—grab it, and file it.

On more specific subjects you face a certain amount of expense. There is no way round it, so concentrate on making your money as effective as possible. You *may* be lucky and find one of the more expensive uniform books in your local lending library; they are starting to carry them, but not so regularly that you can count on it. If you find one which you think will be useful, then take it home whether or not you have a project on the boil. Make a careful list of all the uniforms illustrated in it, and keep the list safe, with a note of the book's title, author, publisher, and shelf-number on the library. Then you can order it with ease next time you really need it. If you have to buy—and all real enthusiasts like to build up a library of their own—then buy wisely. It is going to cost you, but it needn't cost the earth.

Firstly, avoid large, glossy, expensive books which range over the *general* history of uniforms. Take them from the library for a browse, if you like, and note down any useful illustrations, but this kind is little use to the modeller. Identify your area of interest, and while being willing to look into other periods, nationalities, etc, confine your buying to books on your period. You will often be able to borrow something from another modeller who specialises in another period, if you get the urge to step outside home territory once in a while.

Always check over a book carefully before investing; it may not contain the sort of hard information and clear pictures you need, however seductive the title. In stony broke periods we have been known to browse in a far corner of our local bookshop with a pencil and notebook in the pocket — why spend pounds on reference for a single model, if you can take a few quick notes and sketches? Luckily, quite a large number of books for military enthusiasts are now available at under £2, and there are others, a little more expensive, which are really superb value for money if you are really interested in the periods covered.

Apart from the Airfix Magazine Guides, there are two main series you should investigate. Almark Publishing Co Ltd of 49 Malden Way, New Malden, Surrey KT3 6EA, have produced over the past five or six years an enormous range of inexpensive paperbacks on military subjects. Titles of use to modellers of military figures, with several pages of colour illustrations, cover all main periods of interest from Saxon England to Waffen-SS, by way of 18th Century subjects, masses of Napoleonics, and some excellent titles on the First World War. Prices start at about £1.25. Try to get a good look at a copy of whichever title sounds interesting — the quality of the illustrations varies pretty widely; but in general this list is a goldmine for the modeller with a fairly tight budget.

Some 58 titles have now been published in the Men-at-Arms series, by Osprey Publishing Ltd of 12-14 Long Acre, London WC2E 9LP. Current price for these attractive books is £1.75 — and though the authors must declare a personal interest, they are generally acknowledged to be first class value. They comprise about 40 pages of text, about 35 black and white pictures, and eight pages of full colour art of uniformed figures. Again, quality

Another Job study, this time of a 5th Cuirassier taking a peaceful ride. Soldiers spend only a fraction of their lives actually in the presence of the enemy, and modellers should not neglect this fact. The addition of the pipe, and the braiding of helmet-crest and horse's tail, would give any cuirassier model a more tranquil and bucolic look. Note the tied-back corner of the saddlecloth. Remember also that a strong impression of weather can be given to a model by using imagination, and making plumes, coat-tails, horse's mane, flags, and so on all stream in one direction (National Army Museum).

varies, so try to look through the book you want before buying it. The range includes many British regimental histories, and general titles on armies and wars from the Ancient Romans, through medieval subjects, the Seven Years War, the early American wars, the Napoleonic period, the 19th Century Colonial period, up to World War 2. There are also several 'odd-ball' subjects like the Arab Legion and the Cossacks, which make useful reference for original model projects.

Rival publishers regularly eat their hearts out over the prices at which Blandford Press, of 167 High Holborn, London WC1V 6PH, manage to sell their range of uniform books. Most are under £2.00, yet they are packed with colour and information. They have done several Napoleonics, several World War 2 titles, a superb book on the American War of Independence, and titles on 19th Century British and US Civil War uniforms. They often have 80 or so colour pages, with two or three figures on each; although quality of artwork varies from pretty awful to superb, they are generally speaking unrivalled value for money.

A short series of titles on World War 2 subjects—British, American and German—was published a couple of years ago by Arms and Armour Press Ltd, under the title Key Uniform Guides. They didn't have much colour in them, but what there was, was good; and they were packed with informative black and white photos. At 95p they were very good value. No new titles have appeared since the original six, but we still see them on the shelves of newsagents and bookshops; so if you come across them, and 1939-45 is your period, snap them up while you can.

Finally, let us urge you to read the modelling magazines regularly. By cutting up and filing *Airfix Magazine*, *Military Modelling*, and similar journals, you will acquire not only an inexpensive reference library surprisingly fast, but the latest reports on new kits, and many useful articles by experienced modellers on materials and techniques. The small ads in these magazines are also a prime source of specialised tools and materials, often only available by mail order, or difficult to order through shops in many parts of the country.

The basic figure

The purpose of this chapter is to 'talk through' the making and painting of two models—one infantry and one cavalry—exactly as they come from the kit packet, using (with one tiny exception) only those items included in the kit, and painting them according to the colour scheme shown on the kit instruction sheet. The sequence will be described in detail, with suitable notes on points of difficulty, useful techniques, and so on. This chapter is aimed at the novice in this field of modelling, and experienced veterans can skip it if they wish.

Rifleman, 95th Rifles, 1815

We selected the kneeling figure option for our model from this kit, as we had plans to incorporate it in a duo 'mini-diorama' later—see Chapter 4.

First, after spreading the sprues out on our bench and examining parts and instruction artwork to check that all were present and undamaged, we separated the two halves of the torso from the sprue (nos 1 and 2). When doing this, *always* cut with a sharp blade rather than twisting and breaking the parts free. Cut the stalk a little space away from the surface of the moulding, then trim the stub off with your blade and clean up the attachment point, where a blister of broken plastic will naturally be found. Offer up the two parts to check fit—once in ten thousand times some freak mistake may distort a moulding—and if all is well, paint the edges of both parts with liquid cement and press them together. Hold them tightly for a few seconds before setting down to dry. (Take care

not to get liquid cement on your fingers, or this pressure will melt the surface of the polystyrene and immortalise your finger-prints in your model's chest!)

Cut the kneeling legs from their sprue (nos 3 and 4) and clean attachment points. Next, scrape the fine moulding lines from the surface. These run up the front and rear centre of the legs. Place the knife at right-angles to the lines, and lean the top of the blade towards you; then scrape towards yourself. This removes the plastic without risking cutting into it and raising a 'divot'. Don't forget to remove the mould lines from the front and back of the foot as well. Clean up the result with a round-faced file. Next scrape and file away the prominent welt moulded down the outside seam of each trouser leg; this is incorrect for the 95th Rifles. It's quite

Head-on view of the Rifleman. The cord effect on the shako furniture was heightened by using dark green as ground colour and then painting over the high points with light green.

The completed model posed on a base with a little scenic material in the way of pebbles and grass. Note light highlighting of creases; the body of this model was painted with Rose water-colours, and the face with Campaign oil-based posters, for a contrast in texture.

substantial and will take a bit of carving away at some points. As a result you will almost certainly spoil some of the fold detail moulded into the trousers. This must be replaced with a rat-tail file after the trimming is complete. Be careful to file in the areas and directions which emphasise and extend the moulded creases, not at an unrealistic angle to them. Inspect the right foot critically; in this pose the sole of the boot will be visible, and it may need some trimming to a perfect shape and finish. When satisfied with the appearance of both legs, paint both attachment surfaces with liquid cement and press together, wriggling slightly to ensure a well-seated join. Try to line up the folds across the groin, but don't go mad—you'll be working on this area later. When you set the legs to dry, if you put them in a kneeling position, you may notice that the right knee seems a trifle high, making the model lean to the right. Don't worry about this, we will correct it when fixing to the base.

Taking the torso, remove any join lines on the shoulders and ribs by filing across the line with a rounded file; go slowly and carefully. Turning to the rear of the torso, take a flat-faced file and rasp away the surface of the turnbacks until they are only slightly proud of the rear of the coat. They are moulded far too thick—remember that this is only two thicknesses of serge, not a couple of wooden planks. Turn the torso between your fingers as you file, so that the new surface follows the rounded shape of the hip, and does not have a series of flat facets. Don't worry about filing off the moulded lace detail round the edge, this will be painted in later. When this is finished you may notice two slight imperfections, where the vertical join lines cross the top part of the turnbanks. Taking a small

We departed from the kit instructions in one respect only—the painting of the name on the canteen. We find individual touches like this pleasing, but there is no right and wrong about it—some modellers prefer to stick to 'the book' at all times. Remember to set knapsacks slightly tilted, rather than exactly parallel to the ground; they are slung on human shoulders, which are always slightly out of level except when standing to attention.

paintbrush and your jar of 'soup', apply tiny smears and blobs of 'soup' to these areas until the surface is built up to a smooth finish. Put on a bit too much, and file down when it is dry. (It cannot be repeated too often—use 'soup' *sparingly*.) If the joins on ribs, collar, or shoulders require it, paint on smears of 'soup' here as well. Paint across the line to be disguised, 'fairing in' at each end of the streak of 'soup' so that you don't create new and unrealistic blemishes in the form of great proud blobs on the surface. Set the torso aside to dry, lying on its front so as not to disturb the 'soup'.

Returning to the legs, you will find a prominent 'gutter' between the two mouldings running down the 'fly' and between the legs. This must be destroyed—trousers of the period had no central fly but rather a square flap whose vertical edges were placed about three or four inches each side of the centre-line. Working with the rat-tail file, emphasise the creases which cross the centre join line; these are wide and shallow on the right thigh, getting closer together and more marked as they travel diagonally upwards across the groin to the left hip. Use the file in this direction, ie with the fine point moving up towards the left hip. When you've made a clear pattern with the file, take your 'soup' and paint a streak along the 'gutter' between the legs to fill it in. When it is dry, paint across the groin in the same direction as the moulded creases, building up the ridges and avoiding filling in the valleys. Allow this to dry, then work on the area again with the file. You may have to repeat the whole process; but in the end, if you are patient, you should have the legs perfectly faired into one another, with no central gutter, and with realistic transverse creases. In drying periods, you can be cutting the arms (nos 19 and 27) from the sprue, scraping off the moulding lines, and then restoring the surface of the creases with a rat-tail file. When torso 'soup' is dry, take a file and burr down the rather too prominent buttons all over; we want them to stand proud enough to show up when painted, but

they are too big as moulded. At the same time, file completely flat the bottom button in each of the three rows. When both torso and trousers are dry and ready, stick the torso and pelvis together after offering up to ensure the correct angle. Put aside to set firm.

Taking the head (no 23) from the sprue, carefully scrape off the moulding lines which run up obliquely below the ears, and cement it in place in the shallow cone of the collar opening of the torso. Ensure the right angle—looking slightly to his left. Use the liquid cement sparingly in the collar—you don't want to melt the thin edges of the 'cloth' so that they collapse. While this dries, you can work on the shako; it can in fact be added at any stage, since it doesn't interfere with any later stage of the model. Cut body and peak of the shako from the sprue, being particularly careful not to damage the delicate peak. Holding this with tweezers—but not so tightly that it squirts out to be lost forever on the floor!—file the edge of the peak to a perfectly rounded shape; as moulded, it is a bit angular. You may find that one end of the crescent of vertical headband moulded integrally with the peak is too long; equalise this with a knife, or you'll find that when you stick it to the shako the asymmetrical shape pushes the peak awry. Scrape and file away the moulding lines running up the front, across the top and down the back of the shako body, taking care not to damage the little tuft. There are two prominent attachment blisters on this piece, which should be trimmed away. Cement the shako body to the head; then cement the peak to the body. When dry, you can add the cockade and badge. Exercise enormous care when cutting these tiny pieces (nos 24, 25, 26) from the sprue; leave them until you actually need them, and handle with tweezers.

At this point cut the waistbelt from the plastic card provided, using the template on the instruction sheet (part D). (The bottom buttons on the tunic were destroyed so that the belt would lie close—cloth and flesh compress, but polystyrene doesn't.) Using the minimum of cement, stick one end of the belt to the front centre of the waist of the tunic. When it is dry, lead it round the waist with tweezers, pulling gently to keep it taut, and cement the other end in place over the first end at the front. Press gently with a cocktail stick to keep the tension on the belt while this dries. Cut the buckle (no 13) from the sprue, and file the back surface of it to make it thinner; then cement it in place on the front of the belt. Cut free the bullet pouch (no 11), scrape and file off the moulding lines, and stick it in place on the right of the buckle. Always use liquid cement particularly meanly when working with plastic card—it melts easily. When this stage is dry, take the ready-trimmed arms and cement them to the shoulders, at the correct angle; check this against the instruction sheet. (Note that when making our model we deliberately let the arms 'droop' a fraction, to give the final effect of a man raising or lowering his rifle to the aiming position or from it; in our view the finished model looks more natural this way, as it is very hard to get the totally 'compressed' tense look about the neck and shoulders of a man actually firing.) When the arms are firm-set, file the joins to ensure proper fairing in with the torso; pay attention to the rear shoulder, where the cloth would not stand proud at the shoulder seam since it would be tightly stretched. Paint the joins with 'soup' to complete the process of camouflaging the line. While the arms dried, we turned our attention to the accoutrements, which gave us plenty to think about.

The kit illustration shows these in what we consider an unrealistic sequence. It appears that the Rifleman put on first his knapsack; then his ammunition pouch; then his haversack and canteen; then the cord sling of his powder-horn. In fact the knapsack was often removed at the beginning of an action or in halts on the march, and no soldier in his right mind would arrange his kit so that it all had to come off every time he slipped his pack off. We

decided a more realistic order would be, first the ammunition pouch bandolier with its powder-horn cord (they were sometimes actually fixed together); then, the haversack and canteen; and finally the knapsack. Which of these passed over, and which under, the buttoned shoulder-straps of the tunic is a question with no one right answer; use your common sense and your imagination when faced with choices like this. We decided that the knapsack would go on over the shoulder-straps, and everything else underneath them; and planned the next stages accordingly. (This business of working out laboriously in advance in what order each piece of a model goes on to the main figure is *absolutely vital*; never *assume* that if you follow the order of the kit instructions it is all going to come out right.)

Comparing the plastic card sheet with the kit template (E), cut your ammunition pouch bandolier. Work out exactly where the pouch is going to hang on the rear right hip, and cement one end of the bandolier to the jacket at that point, at an angle which will allow it to be passed across the chest to the left shoulder. When it is dry, pull it across the chest with tweezers and note which tunic buttons it covers; then let it go, and with a sharp knife-point remove these buttons. (The angle will vary slightly with each model, but for what it is worth, on ours the buttons removed were the top one in the left hand row; the second, third and fourth in the centre row; and the fourth, fifth and sixth in the right hand row—'his' left and right in each case.) Take the strap in your tweezers again and lead it up across the chest and shoulder, securing it with a tiny smear of cement on the point of the shoulder; then down the back, cementing the end on top of the end already stuck down to the tunic. Trim any excess with a knife-point and leave to dry, while you take the cartridge pouch (no 8) from the sprue and clean it up. Cement it on top of the strap ends, hiding them. At this point the thread for the powder-horn cord should be added. We happened to have a bit of the most useful belting material supplied in Historex kits; this is a strip of 'corduroy', which can be split into threads and peeled apart, ensuring exactly equal width. Ordinary nylon thread would do as well. Take a generous length and pass it over the shoulder, lying along the surface of the ammunition pouch bandolier and secured to it with a tiny smear of cement here and there; let the ends dangle for now.

Next, the bayonet. Cut it from the sprue, trim with care, and cement to a little length of plastic card 'frog' (parts no 12 and F). When dry, cement the frog to the waistbelt on the front of the left hip. Take care with the angle, in this kneeling position the bayonet will lean outwards at top or bottom, with the tip touching the ground. Place it well back against the front edge of the jacket turnback.

Cut the haversack (no 15) from the sprue and trim it. We dislike the method of fixing the strap to two moulded stubs on this part. Instead we cut the stubs off, and filed a little flat strip into the top of each *side* edge of the haversack moulding. Then we cut our strap (template G) and cemented one end to one of these flat areas. When it was set we cemented the haversack in place on the hip of the jacket, and left it to dry while we did some work on the canteen. When the strap was firm we pulled it across the chest and repeated the button-trimming process described above; then cemented it on the right shoulder, and finally to the other side edge of the haversack.

The Rifleman kit has an undetailed canteen moulding (no 16); if you don't have one of the later canteens, such as that from the American Soldier 1775, in your spares box, then scribe and file in some wood detail. Notch the circular standing rim all round; and high on each side, between strap attachments and neck, file across the thickness of the moulding to stimulate the little wooden planks from which it was made. Scribe two or three horizontal or diagonal lines across the face, for the same reason. Cement your strap to one attachment, let it dry, then stick the

canteen on the outside of the haversack and repeat the process described above for the haversack strap. Template H in the kit gives you dimensions for the strap; we find working with plastic card in this sort of size most difficult, as the cement melts it almost every time, so we used a triple thickness of our Historex belting thread.

When the accoutrements are complete and setting, take the shoulder-straps from the sprue (nos 9 and 10) and, holding carefully with tweezers, file their undersides away until they are as thin as you dare make them. Paint the underside with cement, then press them in place on the shoulders one at a time, compressing the straps which pass beneath them as much as you can. While they set, work on the knapsack; separate and trim up the pack and the bedroll (nos 17 and 18) and cement them together, lining up the moulded strap detail. Set aside for painting; they will be stuck on to the back of the model after the painting stage.

Take templates A, B and C and cut card to size. Cement one end each of straps A and B behind the shoulder of the figure, at an angle which will allow them to be pulled down round the shoulder and under the armpit again. Cement them well in towards the spine so that they will be covered by the knapsack. When dry, pull them down and round the shoulder with tweezers, keeping tension as well as you can, and stick the other ends to the back again, below the first ends. When dry, add the cross-strap uniting them across the chest. Next, cut the powder-horn cord to the correct length with scissors. Remove from the sprue and file clean the horn itself; then cement it to the ends of the thread. It's best to coat the thread ends with liquid cement, let it get tacky, then place a minute blob of cement at each attachment point of the horn and offer it up to the thread ends in tweezers. After it catches, add another couple of blobs, then set the model aside and allow ten minutes to dry thoroughly.

At this point we have a model

complete except for hands, rifle, sling, and assembled pack. Take the hands off the sprue and clean them up. Check that no flash is in the way of their eventual grip of the rifle. When satisfied, cement the left hand to the wrist, checking the angle carefully. While it sets, remove and trim up the Baker rifle. You now have a choice. You can stick the right hand to the wrist, or to the rifle. If you adopt the former course you will have the Devil's own job of getting at the chest detail during painting; if the latter, you must be extremely careful to get the angles of hand, rifle and wrist lined up correctly. We chose to stick hand to rifle, and checked angles first by sticking the hand in place with a blob of Plasticine. We then slipped the rifle into the left hand and offered up hand to wrist, altering the angle until it was right. Carefully lifting the rifle free again, we quickly sketched the essential placing of thumb and forefinger, removed hand and Plasticine, and replaced the hand on the rifle with a blob of cement in the palm. A load of trouble? Certainly—but what are you doing modelling if you don't like taking trouble over details? Finally, add the rifle sling.

When the model is completed to painting stage, it is a good idea to sit back, have a sandwich, and look it over very critically for details you may have missed. Perhaps the join of shako and hairline could do with a streak of 'soup'; perhaps the wrist buttons could do with a last stroke of the file. When entirely satisfied, cement the figure to its base. Add a little wedge of plastic, cut from a sprue, beneath the right knee to correct the angle of the kneeling figure.

Painting

The make-or-break stage has now been reached: painting your model. This is a vast subject in itself, and we can only cover broad guidelines here. Only practice and experiment will teach you which materials and techniques suit you best and produce the type of finish you require.

A few of the main types of paint

should perhaps be listed. Apart from the specialist plastic enamels, as manufactured by Airfix and several other companies, which suit many people, those who prefer the absolutely matt finish of good quality water-colours, may like to try Rose Paints or Pelican/Plaka Colours, both of which

A very simple conversion described in Airfix Magazine of February 1975 — from an Airfix Imperial Guard Grenadier to a Grenadier of the Garde de Paris battalion which fought in Spain in 1812. The only structural work necessary is to change the motif on the bearskin plate from an eagle to a grenade; to file clean the cartridge pouch lid; and to remove the pigtail. Otherwise it is simply a question of a new paint-job — often the case, considering that the basic uniforms throughout a given army were often differentiated only by small insignia and facing colours. This soldier wears a white uniform with collar, lining, turnbacks, lapels and cuffs of grass green, piped white round the two latter items. Cuff-slashes are white piped with green, and epaulettes scarlet. All buttons are yellow, the sabre-knot and tassel scarlet, and the turnback ornaments white grenades. 'Customising' can take the form of firewood, native sandals, purloined canteens, rags round musket-locks, and so forth.

 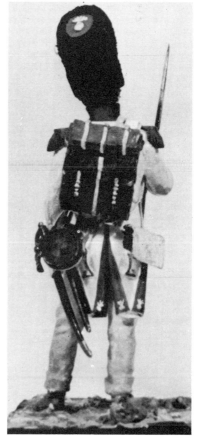

The basic figure

have much to recommend them. Rose paints come in a good range of basic shades; they are infinitely 'mixable'; they can be used in any consistency required, and flow and cover beautifully even when thinned down. Rose's black is extremely good for very fine 'lining' work. The problem of blending an area of shadow or highlight into its base colour is difficult with water-colours, but the 'mixability' and even flow of Rose paints allow the modeller to overpaint the division between two tones of the same colour with thin washes which—with practice—will blur one tone into another very nicely.

The oil-based poster paints in the Campaign Colours range are also very good. They tend not to cover quite as consistently as water-paints, and you may require more than one coat with some subjects. They are good for fine detail work, and particularly good for faces, where highlight, shadow and base colour must be blended imperceptibly.

Some expert modellers prefer true artist's oils, but these take a long time to dry and require a very different technique of application; relatively inexperienced modellers should approach them with caution and experiment at length before attempting a complete paint job on a finished model. Acrylic paints, which are used with water but which dry waterproof, have become increasingly good over the past few years; the range used to be too small and too garish, but George Rowney & Co now make a good spectrum of colours. The two main types are Rowney's Flow Formula Cryla, and Rowney's Acrylic Designer's Gouache. The Cryla (make sure it is Flow Formula that you buy) is easily thinned, or can be used thick from the tube and 'brushed out' like oil paint. It dries waterproof with a slight sheen, and is excellent for horses and, if you like the finish, faces. The Acrylic Designer's Gouache has the same properties as other good-quality gouaches—drying perfectly matt, and thinning nicely with water—except that it dries waterproof, a useful 'safety' feature. Many modellers swear by it for figure painting. Carefully tested combinations made by mixing Flow Formula Cryla and Designer's Gouache allow the painter to produce a range of slightly varying textures and sheens.

Brushes should be the best you can afford—sable if possible. They don't have to be the tiniest on the market, as long as you maintain a good point. Wash them carefully, and when setting aside at the end of a job reform the point by passing them lightly over damp soap. Don't forget to wash this out before use! Dry gently with a soft cloth, always in the direction of the point. And when the point finally collapses on you, break the brush, use the handle as a stirring-rod, and buy a new one—to keep a less than perfect brush in use is a false economy.

Note that polystyrene figures will require undercoats when you use watercolours or acrylics. The best undercoat is a thin application of matt oil-based paint such as one of the Campaign range, or a thinned matt enamel (we find spray-cans invaluable for this chore.) The idea is to seal the surface without blocking up any of the fine surface detail. When a figure has been modified in any way, such as by changing animation or filling areas of the surface with putty, the final undercoat is also very useful in showing up immediately areas where the surface needs more attention for perfect 'continuity'.

So, back to our Rifleman:

First we undercoated with a pale grey matt Airfix enamel. When it was dry, we tackled the trickiest area first—the face. If it is painted first, and comes out well, the psychological effect is good: it encourages you ('If I can do that, I can do *anything*'), and makes you particularly careful and deliberate about the rest of the painting, so anxious are you to avoid spoiling a model now promising so well! On a more practical level, it means that you can twist and turn and brace and rest the figure in any position you need during this taxing job, without danger of finger-marking any painted areas. We used Campaign Colours, but for the purposes of describing the

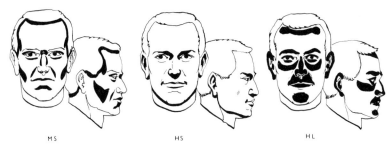

MS   HS   HL

Stages in face painting: medium and heavy shadow areas, and main highlights.

process we will describe shades in general terms, so that modellers using different mediums can 'translate' as they go along.

You need your basic flesh tone; shadow, from light to dark; and highlight, from strong to faint. Put out small quantities of your basic shades on the plate, card, or whatever you use as a palette, and mix in the middle as required. The best way to make basic flesh tone is to start with white and add ochre and red until you get what you want. For a dark-skinned soldier you should start with ochre and red until you get what you want. For a dark-skinned soldier you should start with ochre and add red and brown; for shadow add red and/or brown to the basic mix until you get the required depth; for dark-skinned subjects, a little dark green will give the desired effect. For highlight, a little basic flesh in a pool of white will give you a good shade; for dark-skinned subjects, add ochre to white.

We painted the eyeballs first, applying the white without worrying how much we overran onto the lids. Then we added blue irises to each eye, making the circle of blue overlap the edge of the lid top and bottom; they should be in line with the corners of the mouth. Purists can then add a tiny drop of black to the centre of the blue, for the pupils. When this was dry, we painted in the edges of the lids; red-brown lines, as fine as possible, along the bottom lids, and dark brown along the top lids. We then painted the whole eye sockets in medium shadow. When

this was finished we painted in the whole face in basic flesh tone.

Next we added the areas of medium shadow, and blended their edges into the basic tone. These are the sides of the nose; the L-shaped shadows under the cheekbones; the underside of the nose; the underside of the bottom lip; the line where the neck meets the collar; the hairline all round; the back of the ear, and the inside of the ear; and the undersurface of the jaw. (If your model is to be bare-headed, the hollows of the temples should also be lightly shaded and the eyebrow ridge highlighted.)

Light highlight should be added to the upper plane of the cheekbones; the upper lip; the point of the chin; and the jawline. Strong highlight goes down the top of the nose, and on the bulges of the nostrils; at the outer ends of the cheekbones; and around the rim of the ear. Dark shadow appears under the centre of the jaw; under the earlobe; in the nostrils; in lines where the bulge of the nostril meets the face; in lines downward and outward from the nostril, passing outside the corners of the mouth; in the centre hole of the ear; and in the corners of the mouth.

The vital areas of eye and mouth should be considered with great care. Our eye socket is now completely in medium shadow, with the actual eyeball painted and outlined. Dark shadow must be added to the inner corner of the eye socket, curving up and out a short way across the upper limit of the lid, ie immediately below the eyebrow ridge. Medium highlight must

The basic figure

now be added to the outer half of the bulge of the upper lid. A fine line of medium highlight can also be added along the bottom lid immediately below the dark line edging the eyeball. (This sounds complicated, but the simplest way to grasp it is to look at your own eye in a mirror.) As for the mouth, you want above all things to avoid a bright 'lipsticked doll' appearance. Paint the underside of the top lip with medium shadow, tending towards red rather than brown. Paint the top surface of the bottom lip with medium highlight with a touch of light red. The fine line separating the lips should be dark brown, or a mixture of red and black.

Hair should be painted in a basic shade first, and then with a darker shade of the same colour at the base of the skull, behind the ears, and on rear and lower edges of the sideburns. If the hair is prominently modelled, you can highlight simply by passing an almost-dry brush loaded with a lighter tone of your basic shade across the surface, so that it is picked up only by the 'ridges'. Add a little extra highlight down the front edges of the sideburns by stroking lightly. If the hair is *not* prominently modelled, then make sure it is! The point of a craft-knife applied with care will quickly groove the surface. Short of this, a reasonable effect can be achieved by dabbing on to the hair surface little spots of thick paint such as Rowney Cryla (*not* Flow Formula) and pulling the brush sharply away to 'tag' it. This can look very effective if continued up to and minutely overlapping the headband of a shako at the sides. Let this painted-on hair dry properly before painting with the required colour. You can add moustaches and beards in the same way.

Having finished our face, we now surveyed the rest of the figure. He is completely assembled and under-coated except for the back-pack and rifle. These can be painted separately at any stage while waiting for some part of the main figure to dry. The pack and straps are painted according to the kit instructions. Leave a little strip of the front face of the pack—the face that butts against the back of the man—unpainted, across the lower end; this is to accept the cement. The rifle should be painted first with dark semi-gloss brown, or with matt brown, over all the wooden parts. When dry, paint the metal parts in silver mixed with black, or with gunmetal colour; in the case of the Baker you will need to paint some parts brass as well. When the wood and metal are both dry, go over the rifle again with both colours, painting out accidental overlaps. When these are dry, take your finest-pointed brush and load it with thinned black; apply this in fine lines to all the places where metal and wood join, and around the edges of the hammer, trigger, bayonet-bar, ramrod pipes, and so forth. Finally, if you used matt brown for the wood, overpaint it with Burnt Sienna drawing ink applied sparingly—this gives a nice deep shine. It's a good idea to paint the sling last of all; if you handle it as delicately as you should, and if it has a good generous hanging loop to it, you can hold the rifle by it when painting, thanks to the slight stiffness of the plastic card.

The shako can be painted at any stage you like. For the body, we prefer to paint all the straps and accoutrements first, so that it doesn't matter if a bit of paint slops onto the main figure in the process. When dry, we painted the facings in black and edged them with white, for the same reason. (This way, you only have to worry about one perfect edge—that which is meeting the black areas; it is always simpler to straighten the other edge of a width of piping, etc, by painting up to it with your main shade, than to apply it perfectly straight on both edges between two areas of main colour.)

We then painted the torso, arms and legs in rifle green, sweeping it carefully up to the edges of all straps, facings, etc, with the side of a steadily-held brush. We then darkened the pool of green with black, and applied it in the obvious shadow areas—folds of knee and elbow, the underside of the upper arms, the underside of the left thigh, the crease under the buttocks, etc.

These were gently blended into the surrounding areas of base green by stroking the meeting-lines with an almost dry, clean brush. Note that a brush with too much thinners on it will pick up paint—go *delicately*. Then we considered the highlights. Since the subject is in dark green, highlighting should be minimal—in our opinion, at least; some modellers like dramatic contrasts, and are of course at liberty to strive for whatever effect they like. Adding a *trace* of white to our pool of green, we very sparingly highlighted only the most obviously 'rucked-up' folds of arms and legs, and blended it in,

We then took our matt black, thinned right down, and carefully added a tiny drop to each moulded button, allowing it to spread *just* outside the edge of the moulded buttons. When dry, we applied a tiny drop of silver to each button, leaving a fine circle of black showing round the edge. This is hardly visible against the dark green, but in fact throws the buttons up nicely. With the same thinned black, we then painted the finest lines we could manage along the meeting areas of colour. This means, the front join of the jacket; where the green of the jacket and the white edge of the turnbacks, cuffs and shoulder-straps meet; where green jacket and cross-straps for haversack and canteen meet; down the outer seams of the overalls; and where the wrists and ankles meet the cuffs and trouser-bottoms. We then painted the hands, left until now because so many loaded brushes had been probing between them to get at the torso and rifle. Use basic flesh tone, with medium shadow on the inside surfaces and dark shadow between the fingers and in the creases inside the knuckles; highlight the top surface of the fingers and the knuckle-ridge. Leave a little area of the left palm unpainted, to accept the cement for the rifle. Finally, we painted the gaiters and shoes. If done earlier, they might have been spoiled by brushing finger-tips while we used the base as a 'handle' during painting.

The pack can now be added. When it is set, slip the rifle into the left hand and locate the right hand and wrist. Secure with cement on the wrist 'stump' and in the left palm. Be very careful not to allow the cement to ooze from the right wrist. It remains only to decorate the base with putty 'earth', small pebbles, sisal 'grass', or any other finish you prefer, and to paint it.

Trooper, Bengal Lancers, 1910

The second kit which we made up exactly as the kit instructions, logging our progress, was this handsome new Skinner's Horse mounted figure from Airfix. It captures the pride and colour of the Indian Army very nicely, and the mouldings are very clean. Apart from its primary subject, the kit provides many parts which the experienced modeller will at once recognise as useful additions to the spares box: neatly putteed lower legs, a Martini-action rifle in a scabbard, a nice bamboo lance, and a superbly moulded turbaned head which we feel

Side view of completed Bengal Lancer. The surface textures of horse and rider should vary. We used Campaign oil-based poster colour on the face, Rose water-colour on the uniform, and Flow Formula Cryla paints on the horse.

sure will soon be seen in a number of conversions of other Indian subjects in modelling journals.

After studying the instructions and the sprues carefully, we brought to the modelling bench the best easily-available reference work: A. H. Bowling's *Indian Cavalry Regiments 1880-1914* in the inexpensive Almark series. This has extremely useful photographic and artwork illustrations of this regiment (and will also suggest many conversion ideas—the basic cut of the Indian cavalry uniform did not vary much in most cases, and a series of figures in contrasting and highly coloured uniforms is well within the scope of most modellers using this single kit as a basis). After comparing this reference with the kit, we set to work. Note, incidentally, that with a mounted figure you can naturally save time by working on the horse while the figure dries, then on the figure while the horse sets, then back to the horse, and so forth.

First we took the two halves of the horse body from the sprue, cutting the sprue a little distance from the surface of the horse and then trimming the attachment points with the knife and file. Then we carefully removed the moulding-lines from the horse halves. These will be found going up the front and back of the legs, then in across the stomach towards the centre-line. Scrape these intitially with the side of the blade, the blade being at right angles to the line and the top of the blade leaning in the direction of the scrape. Finish off with a rounded file—you don't want flat areas on a natural subject like a horse's body. Cement the halves together and set aside to dry thoroughly, after holding them for the first minute or so.

Next we trimmed and fitted together the two halves of the rider's torso. There are some very thin places at certain points of the join, so be careful not to trim or file too hard or you'll go through. While this is drying, take from the sprue the horse's head section and ear section. Scrape and file moulding lines off, and cement first the head and then the ears to the neck of the main horse assembly, waiting for the first to

dry before adding the second. Check angles, and continuity of surfaces each side of joins, with great care. Some minor trimming or filling may be necessary. When this stage is set, we faced the major operation of scraping, filing, filling, and re-filing the centre line of the horse's body, which *must* be rendered invisible. At some points saddle and harness will hide the join, but at others you must work patiently to eliminate it. Don't get fed up and move on—an unrealistic 'seam' down your nag's stomach will destroy the authenticity of an otherwise perfect model. In the mane the line shows up badly, because it runs at right-angles to the sideways hang of the mane. You will have to work here with a file, perhaps almost destroying the surface

The use of acrylic paint on the horse, even by horse-modellers as unskilled as the author, will at least give a convincing hairy sheen to the brute's body!

of the mane in your efforts to cover up any slightest section of joint-line. Don't worry about this—you can build the mane up again easily enough by painting across the centre-line with patient applications of 'soup'. When your tool work on the centre-line of the horse is complete, paint over it with 'soup'. Don't simply paint a strip of 'soup' down the line, overlapping on either side—this will make a raised strip when dry, as noticeable and unrealistic as the original centre-line. Paint across the joint, using the 'soup' sparingly, and continuing it down the sides of the back in accordance with the contours of the body. At the same time, fill with 'soup' any unsightly cracks around the edges of head and ear sections. (NB 'soup' should always be used sparingly—because it is in a suspension with a strong solvent base, it can itself melt the surface it is applied to. Put it on in tiny smears, and thin layers. Always let one layer dry before adding another, or you will get a build-up of still-liquid solvent which will eat through your model.)

While the 'soup' dried we took the torso of the man and worked on his joint-line with blade, round-edge and sharp-edge files. Make your file strokes in the direction of the moulded folds and creases, continuing them across the joint-line. Use round-edge files for folded cloth areas, and a flat-face blade for such areas as the belt. When you've achieved what you can with tools, apply your 'soup'; use a little at a time, and again, paint in the direction of the moulded folds, building up 'peaks' and being careful not to fill 'valleys' too full of 'soup', so that you enhance rather than destroy the moulded detail. Work with particular care on the side surfaces of the standing collar—a tell-tale line often shows up here; and a dip sometimes appears in the top line where the two halves of the collar meet, which must be built up with a tiny blob of 'soup'. At some point while working on the torso, file down the surface of the cross-belt where it passes over the shoulder: we have a chain-mail epaulette to add here, and it shouldn't stand up too proud.

At this point we started work on the saddle. We took it from the sprue, trimmed it, and cemented the two halves together. Here we encountered trouble. On the early pre-production pressing we were working from, the two halves did not fit well together and did not match the angle of the horse's back, the flaps sticking out sideways at much too great an angle. As the saddle was so admirably thinly moulded it was impossible to work on it in isolation without risk; so we had to cement it to the horse at this early point, and work on it in situ. This is undesirable—really the ideal is to cement as little as possible of the saddlery to a horse before the painting stage; but we had no choice. We bent the flaps down and stuck them to the horse's barrel, softening them carefully with liquid cement on the inner surface; then we had to work long and delicately on the centre-line of the saddle, filling the resultant gap with 'soup', filing and trimming, to produce an unbroken surface. We added the cinch or girth at the same time. Note, incidentally, that the open backs of the saddle-wallets show rather badly; it is worth filling them in with putty and making a smooth rear surface, skinning it when dry with 'soup' to make a uniform painting surface.

While the saddle dried and recovered from all the frantic activity, we trimmed and filed the beautifully moulded lower legs of the rider, in puttees and spurred boots. Remember that on a mounted model the feet show much more clearly than on an infantryman, so check the shape and finish of the boots carefully, trimming and filing the bottom and edge of the sole if necessary. Check the fit of the stirrup-irons at this point; you don't want to find that the feet don't fit into them when assembling painted sections of the model. We then stuck the lower legs to the knees, and while still tacky, slipped the figure into the saddle to confirm the angle of the lower legs.

We then took the two halves of the turbaned head, and trimmed them before cementing together. This is a beautifully delicate moulding and must

The basic figure

be worked on very slowly with a light hand. Scrape the moulding line and joint-line off, and add 'soup' in tiny streaks and blobs to complete the camouflage. When dry, the head was added to the neck of the torso; this is not a very strong joint, and thus you should be careful to complete all filing and trimming work on the head before putting it in place. Note that it should look slightly to the rider's right, and is set well back. The hanging tail of the turban can be added when the neck is set firm; check the kit illustrations for position, and support it with a blob of Plasticine (well away from the cementing area) while it dries.

Taking the arms, we scraped off moulding-lines, being careful not to damage the line of piping down the back-seams; and cemented them to the shoulder, making sure that the piping on arms and rear torso met neatly behind the shoulder. We checked that the right hand fitted the grip of the lance, before final cementing; slipping the lance through the hand and resting its butt outside the boot in the position it would adopt, we then applied the cement and stuck the arm to the shoulder, leaving the lance in place during drying so that the arm could not slip out of the required angle.

While the rider dried we returned to the horse, did some final work on the saddle, and added the tail. We then finished off the arm-joints of the rider, using a rat-tail file and a blade, and finally trickling a little 'soup' into the joint, to fair arm and body together convincingly. We then added the pouch to the right front of the belt, and the epaulettes to the shoulders. The rider was now complete. At a suitable moment we undercoated him, and his still-separate lance, leaving a bare patch in the right palm and on the lance grip. We undercoated the horse at this point, and in due course painted him (see below). Before finally painting the rider we took a piece of sprue and stuck it vertically up into his crutch, securing with a *small* blob of cement. This makes a handle for holding the rider by during painting; it can be cut off when he is complete and ready for adding to

the saddle, and the mark will be hidden when he is in place. At various stages during painting of horse and man, we removed the remaining pieces of equipment and harness from the sprue, trimmed them, and painted them. When horse and rider were dry we 'furnished' the horse, scraping a little patch of plastic free from paint where necessary with the tip of a knife. This may seem a cack-handed way of going about it, but it is just not possible to do a good job of painting the horse with all those scabbards and straps in the way. It is hard enough to paint the straps neatly when they are in place, without slopping over onto the horse; to paint a completely assembled model from scratch is a task you should avoid. When all is dry, cement the rider into the saddle, cement the lance into his right hand, and slip the reins through

It is quite impossible to get a true scale effect when painting the striped pagri—in the original, some of the stripes are only a quarter-inch wide. A pleasing effect can still be achieved by painting the general character of the design, which is perfectly feasible in 54mm scale.

his left. The kit includes a moulded loop of hanging rein, but we preferred to discard this and pass the actual loop of plastic card rein through the hand, folding it over and securing with a tiny drop of cement on the back of the hand; the difference in section between card reins and moulded loop will inevitably show, and we didn't like the idea.

Painting

There is nothing special to add about the job of painting the rider, beyond what was said in the last section; obviously the complexion of the rider must be dark, and shadows and highlights should be added by mixing dark green and ochre into your basic flesh mix. The chain epaulettes can be painted first with black, which is brushed well into the crevices and indentations of the surface. When it is dry, paint over the epaulette with a lightly loaded brush of silver, just catching the high spots, so as to leave the black visible between; this will accentuate the texture of the chain. Check your kit illustrations and your reference book throughout painting, and let each stage dry before tackling the next.

On the question of the horse's paint job there is more to say. Painting horses is to some modellers a delight, to others a torture. To be absolutely honest, we fall into the latter category. To the authors, a horse is a large and stupid beast, dangerous at both ends, unpredictable at all times, and subject to a thousand diseases with sinister names like 'thrips' and 'staggers' and what-have-you. More to the immediate point, never having had much to do with the jug-headed monsters, the authors' ignorance of the muscle-structure of a horse is sublime. And when you are painting a model horse, that is a problem. So there follow a couple of brief hints for modellers as innocent of horse-lore as ourselves.

For painting the brute, use Rowney's Flow Formula Cryla. It dries with that slight sheen which is correct for a horse's coat, and contrasts pleasantly with the matt of the rider's uniform. It dries quickly and is easy to use. Surround yourself with colour photos of horses in all types of stance and movement, and of all colours; do not forget close-ups of the head, for muzzle and eye detail. These photo-references may be obtained cheaply and simply by buying magazines which cater for the countryman and the pony-club types in your local newsagent. Isolate the references which come nearest to the stance of your model and the preferred colour of your horse, and study them at length until you can identify *exactly* the areas of highlight and shadow, medium and strong, all over the head, legs and body.

Do not start the paint job with an overall basic shade, working in highlights and shadows later, as you would with a soldier. Begin by painting the working area (say, one quarter of the beast at a time) in the necessary shades of medium highlight and medium shadow, blending the two together—this blending will form the 'basic shade' in those areas where it would naturally appear. (Remember that the upper part of the body will tend to be lighter overall, and the belly and lower flanks darker overall.) Then your strong shadows and highlights go on, and are blended at the edges. The area of the muzzle and around the eye will usually be a pinkish grey, but not always—go by your colour reference photos. The dark eye itself should have a very liquid look; add varnish to the finished area. Follow the fine moulded details of veins and tendons with your highlighting and shadowing. If possible, get hold of good colour photos of model horses finished by modellers of great skill; your monthly journal may offer these, or some publication such as the Historex catalogue—this latter is really excellent. Study such photos, and copy the techniques you identify. When working with well-moulded models you do have the advantage that the paint will naturally tend to puddle in depressed areas and thin out as you brush it over proud areas, thus acting as an automatic guide to shadowing and highlighting.

The basic figure

three

Simpler conversions

The simplest conversion of all is that which involves no structural changes, but merely a new paint job. The amount of difference can vary from the 'promotion' of a model by painting on corporal's chevrons, to a quite ingenious and radical change involving two types of soldier with uniforms of the same cut but completely different colours. Ideas will occur to you as you study your reference books and files. The avid converter will acquire an eye which notices at once a subject which attracts him and is similar in basic outlines to a kit readily available. The hobby magazines frequently run articles devoted to this kind of project; and it is not hard to become addicted to 'pitting your wits' against the manufacturers, as it were!

Within any given army and period the possibilities are usually quite wide. Most armies have always adopted a basic cut of uniform with minor variations between, at least, regiments within the infantry and foot artillery, and regiments within the mounted branch. Within any given Line Infantry branch the variations between uniforms from regiment to regiment have usually been minimal, often limited to facing colours only. In Chapter 4 we describe the possiblities of converting Airfix's 1815 Coldstream Guardsman and 95th Rifleman into Line soldiers of the Napoleonic Wars; and later in this chapter we suggest simple conversions from the Afrika Korps Multipose set into other German World War 2 subjects. We start, however, with an even simpler project; the alteration of Airfix's superb new French Foreign

Legion kit by means of painted insignia and an 'individualised' pack alone. (We might add that this kit, which reaches new standards of moulding quality, offers the keen converter many seductive alternatives for more radical exercises. With a little work, a few bits from the spares box, and a Rose head in an Adrian helmet, it becomes a *poilu* of 1915-18. The head recalls at once various Indian Mutiny types of the British and Indian Armies. The basic leg and foot shapes have a multitude of uses, from British infantry of the Victorian colonial period to Tommies of World War 2. The rifle could be the basis for many bolt-action designs of the early 20th Century.)

Sergent, Foreign Legion, 1908

The first step is to assemble your references. The Legion is a passion of the author's, so this was no problem. The references used were a number of photographs from various sources, including one reproduced herewith and some which appear in Airfix Magazine Guide No 13; back numbers of *Képi Blanc* magazine; issue 29 of *Gazette des Uniformes*; and a book of uniform regulations. The finished figure depicts a man from the 2ᵉ Régiment Etranger in Morocco.

First we carried out some minor corrections to the mouldings. The képi peak should be rounded, so we filed the corners off carefully. The shape should be more sloped forward, so we filed down the front part to get nearer the shape of, for instance, a US Civil War cap, though not quite so pronounced as that. The upper rim was filed to give a softer, more rounded-over shape. The Lebel rifle seems to have acquired an odd lump beneath the lock immediately forward of the trigger guard; this should be trimmed off, making the lower line of the stock quite level and smooth from trigger guard forwards. The ammunition pouches had gussets in the side and bottom surfaces, and these are easily filed in with the edge of a triangular-section file. The canteen necks are both too long and too thick, we cut them back by the length of the

Group of légionnaires near Figuig, 1911. On the left is a sergent*—note single gold rank stripe and gold piping round cuff. The leather gaiters were not always worn—these soldiers have the white trousers simply bloused at the ankle. NB unlike the kit artwork, badges were never worn with the white képi cover.*

stoppers, filed them thinner, and filed in new grooves to indicate the corks. We also added a putty beard to the jaw.

Other structural changes were limited to the pack. It ought to have another pair of stowage straps round the 'shoulders' of the tent roll, high up on each side level with the top of the big mess-tin. We carefully filed grooves here, to accept new straps from lengths of plastic card sheet, supplied with the kit. The pair of tent-poles should be given another little collar of plastic card strap, level with the new stowage strap when fixed to the pack. Just above this, we wound a thread a few times round the poles, and round a

Position of Légion insignia of rank, long service, and marksmanship on left arm of coat—here, a corporal with more than ten years' service.

'tent-peg' of conventional shape carved from scrap sprue. A spare pair of boots came next, an easy addition but one which gives a nice operational look to the pack. Taking a spare pair of legs from the oddments box, we cut off the feet just above the boot-soles, about level with the top of the insteps. These were cleaned up with the file, and then given little straps around the bottom of the instep, like the retaining straps of Napoleonic gaiters but of the same width as the pack stowage straps. The boots were then stuck to the rear face of the knapsack on each side of the mess-tin, as if the 'uppers' and ankle parts had been flattened and thrust into the vertical crevice between pack sides and tent-roll; the instep straps should be level with the lower horizontal stowage straps of the roll, the toes upwards, the soles outwards. It doesn't matter if the big mess-tin pushes them into untidy angles—so much the better and more realistic. Lastly, we made a bundle of kindling wood from tiny bare branches of lichen and odd twig-ends from a dead houseplant, and tied it with thread. After the pack is painted, this can be added horizontally above the big

Simpler conversions

Partly completed Légion figure. The main assembly is complete, and for ease of handling has been stuck to the base (already treated with putty and sand) before 'soup' is applied to the join lines. Leaning against the figure is the modified knapsack, with tent-peg and guy-cords, extra straps, and spare boots; at painting stage the latter will be hob-nailed.

Conversion idea—why not turn the Légion kit into a poilu of 1914 or 1915? At the beginning of the war the coat was dark blue-grey, the képi had a blue-grey cover, and the trousers were red. By 1915 the army was in horizon blue coats, trousers, and képi-covers, with puttees instead of leather gaiters. Personal equipment is identical to that of the légionnaire in the kit, or very easily modified from it. This picture gives a good idea of the general effect.

mess-tin, held by the vertical central stowage strap as it passes down over the mess-tin. The only other structural addition to the kit was a mug slung on the canteen strap; this came from the Historex spares sprue of cooking and eating utensils, no 463—an invaluable addition to the spares box, which only costs pennies.

Paint your model largely as the kit instructions. You might note that collar insignia seems to have varied; some soldiers wore the regimental number in dark blue, almost invisible on the dark RAF blue of the coat; others seem to have worn it in red. Rank and service chevrons can be added to the sleeve to taste. These comprised diagonals on the forearms, from just above the cuff at the front to just below the elbow at the back; and inverted chevrons on the upper left arm only. Rank stripes and 'hash marks' were always in the same colour—gold for sergeants and up, red for senior privates and corporals. A thin line of piping round the top of the cuff followed the same colour sequence. Below the service chevrons sometimes appeared a little cloth *cor-de-chasse* in red, silver or gold, for the three ascending classes of marksmanship award. We gave our légionnaire a *sergent's* single gold diagonal on each forearm, two gold chevrons indicating ten years' complete enlistment, and a 1st Class Marksman's bugle-horn in gold. Gold insignia stand out better if you paint them first in matt black, then go over them in gold leaving a minute rim of black all round.

Gunner, Royal Artillery, 1812-15

Thanks to the general similarity of British infantry and artillery tunics in the Napoleonic period, you can make a very acceptable artilleryman from the 42nd Highlander, Coldstream Guard, and Rifleman kits in the Airfix range. This will also allow the modeller to use some imaginative 'props' and animation. We decided to pose our artilleryman in a working party situation, helping to clear out a wrecked French battery after its capture, perhaps. Wellington's army never had enough 'pick-and-shovel' hands available; and even in the late stages of the Peninsular War, when larger detachments of sappers and miners became available, infantry and gunners had to bear a hand with entrenching, building batteries, etc. Our gunner may be clearing up after one of the positional battles in the south of France in 1814.

Take the standing legs from the Rifleman and join them. Take the 42nd Highlander torso halves, and carve away the obstructions at the bottom of the front half, just as in our conversion of the kneeling redcoat at Waterloo (see Chapter 4). Carefully join the torso halves, and the torso to the legs. As with the kneeling figure, build up the stomach below the jacket with putty and/or 'soup'. Do your filing and trimming carefully, as the join at the waist is rather weak and won't stand rough handling. When everything is finshed, and dried, add the Coldstream head and shako to the torso. You will have to cut off the neck from the head,

The completed Royal Artillery gunner, 1815, wielding his pick amid the rubble. No painting has yet been done.

as it won't fit the hole. Cement in place carefully—it is at moments like this that liquid cement really shows its advantages. Add the shako cords, badge and tuft, just as in the Coldstream kit instructions. If you like to add that individual touch, then before sticking head and shako in place, give the shako a rakish tilt over one eyebrow by carefully filing the top surface of the head down a bit at one side. A sliver of putty, or a little smear of 'soup', can be added at the joint of shako and head on the high side after cementing, to fill any unrealistic hairline gap. This filling should be made to look like hair.

You can choose your arms according to the position desired, bearing in mind (a) that not *all* the arms in all the kits in the range are interchangeable, and selected limbs should be offered up to check fit before cementing; and (b) that the RA had round cuffs with vertical lace, just like the 42nd Highlanders. We

used the Highlander's arms, nos 27 and 28 on the sprue, as they give a realistic 'pick-axe' position—and, for that matter, a pretty convincing impression of throwing earth over the shoulder from a spade, if you prefer. While the cement of the second arm applied was still tacky, we slipped the pick-axe handle (from Historex spares, again) through both hands to make sure the arms were properly aligned, and left it there while the arm dried. When this stage is complete, add the plain, tufted shoulder straps from the Highlander kit. On fatigues it seemed logical that the gunner would carry only his canteen for occasional 'wets', so we slung this round him as per the kit instructions and ignored the rest of the equipment.

The bucket also came from a Historex sprue, the most useful source of such 'props'. He could also hold a shovel from the same source; or an artillery rammer, or a crow-bar, made from scrap. Contemporary prints in

The model painted, with Historex bucket added in the foreground. Note dust marks on blue jacket—a clean appearance would be quite unconvincing here.

Rear view of the unpainted gunner; the base is built up with crumbled lumps of cement, and wood from scrap shavings, on a modelling putty ground.

Reconstruction of the probable appearance of the rear of an Artillery coatee of 1815—the details of the rear lacing are not confirmed.

vertically from the centre of the bottom of the triangle down the edge of the rear vent to the edge of the skirt. The three-point scalloped pocket is edged *all round* with a frame of yellow braid. It has three yellow buttons, and three bastion-shaped loops from them back almost to the lower, straight edge of the pocket. Since the Highlander's pocket has four, it is advisable to clean off this detail before painting.

The base was made up from a piece of stout plastic as the bottom-board, with 'ground' made from putty. Suitable rocks were pushed into this while tacky, made from bits of smashed cement. A few slivers of splintered wood from an old picture-frame, a scatter of small gravel—*et voilà.*

reference books offer ideas.

The jacket is painted dark blue with red facings on collar, cuffs and shoulder straps. The lace loops are yellow, as is the lacing round the collar and shoulder straps and the tufts on the latter. The turnbacks are white; the tuft on the shako is all white, the cords yellow, and the badge gold. The trousers are the usual British grey campaign garments, the boots black, the spats black or dark grey. The canteen is azure blue with a brown or black strap. The pick handle can be natural wood, the bucket staves the same, or olive green, strapped with dirty black iron. The rear lacing requires care.

The differences between the few contemporary sources of information on this uniform oblige the modeller to pick a version and stick to it. We recommend the following: yellow braid around the edges of the white turnback; a triangle of yellow braid right in the small of the lower back, as on infantry tunics of the day; a single central line of yellow braid dropping

Infantryman, Waffen-SS, 1944

The Airfix Afrika Korps Multipose set is a real treasure-house for figure modellers, offering as it does not just a mass of arms and equipment, but the possibility of whole figures of other branches and periods of the World War 2 German forces. We chose an infantry NCO of the élite and dreaded Waffen-SS, creeping up to the firing line through urban wreckage. This is a simple conversion, whose difference from the subject of the original kit depends almost entirely on painting, but which looks very striking when complete.

We selected parts which would give us an impression of the four-pocket camouflage uniform typical of the Waffen-SS on all fronts at this stage of the war. Take torso no 27 and legs no 30; and with a sharp blade trim off the box-pleat detail from all four pockets. The selection of arms is up to you, depending on the weapon and equipment, and the base scenery. We used right arm no 3, as our soldier is holding his MP 40 sub-machine-gun out of his way as he climbs over a shattered wall. We used left arm no 29, cutting off and re-cementing the hand at a new angle so that he could rest it realistically on the wall as he climbed over it. (We prepared the base in parallel with the figure, using those moments when things were drying on one to work on the other, and were thus able to offer up the figure to his base at various stages and check the angles, etc.) A suitable head, no 26, was now added to the torso.

In this hunched position it would probably be easier to fit rifle ammunition pouches to his belt and arm him with a Mauser K98; but we wanted the sinisterly functional outline of the MP40, so long magazine pouches it had to be. These were worn slanting slightly, the top ends leaning inward toward the middle of the body, but even so we had to position them well back on the hips to fit round his raised thighs. This is quite permissible —remember, the real thing was not soft and crushable, it had six rigid steel magazines in it! Now we added the field assault equipment to the back: mess-tin, rolled camouflage poncho, entrenching-tool (with or without bayonet scabbard, to taste, as sub-machine-gunners sometimes hung on to their bayonets although they could not fit them to the MP40), bread-bag, water canteen and gasmask case. The kit instructions are quite clear on the relative positions of these items, but remember that this is a general guide only—although the mess-tin and poncho had definite places on the assault harness, gas-mask, entrenching tools, bread-bags and canteens were

often slung differently, to individual preference.

We wanted to have our trooper wearing the stylish peaked field-cap, with his helmet slung on his belt over the entrenching tool head. The helmet would have been in a cloth camouflage cover with this uniform; so with patience and care we 'rumpled' and 'lumped' its surface with streaks of plastic 'soup'. This is where photographic reference comes in—it is impossible to describe this sort of effect properly, you must study the real thing. Since the slung helmet was to cover part of the belt equipment we left it off, to cement in place at the last minute, after painting. We also prepared but left off the MP40, as to cement it now could make painting the figure unnecessarily difficult. Next we turned to the field-cap.

The splendid Afrika Korps set castings, with superbly moulded complete heads and 'empty' hats, were welcomed with rapture by conversion-minded modellers; but this style of moulding has certain drawbacks, inevitably. The 'walls' of the hats are really too thick in scale, and the 'holes' a little large, so that if used straight from the sprue they hang on the wearer's ears, giving a gormless effect which is the last thing we want for our leopard-spotted killer here! Now comes a simple but demanding chore. With a

Completed Waffen-SS NCO on his 'urban rubble' base. An American firm, Kurton, have just produced most useful packets of 1:35 scale bricks moulded in clay, but at the time of writing it is not clear how best to obtain these in Britain.

Model Soldiers

fine Swiss file, preferably the triangular-bladed type, we filed all round the outside of the band of the field-cap, thinning out the plastic equally and removing the protruberant 'turn-up' detail completely. Using a photo of the real thing as guide, we worked slowly and delicately, not risking filing right through the plastic at any point, until the outline was as we wanted it. We then cemented it in place, using liquid cement sparingly—it could soften and distort the now-wafer-thin plastic if used with a heavy hand. When it was set, we used droplets of plastic 'soup' around the join of hat and head, building up the hair until a more natural appearance was achieved, without any great overhang under the edge of the cap. Putty, applied in scraps on a knife-blade, would do just as well. The final touch is optional. We had on the bench Armour Accessories' superb Set 4, of beautifully fine moulded German insignia and equipment in 1:35 scale. This is a little small for our 54mm figure on the face of it, but as these tiny flakes of plastic are a shade larger than their nominal scale, the difference is unimportant. We took the SS death's-head badge, and cemented it—with a minute drop of liquid glue—to the front of the cap crown; and the SS eagle badge followed, high on the left hand side of the cap, above the ear. You could paint these badges just as well,

but having the mouldings we couldn't resist using them.

Painting this figure requires colour reference, best obtained either from Osprey's Men-at-Arms book *The Waffen-SS*, or from the excellent book of the same title in the Almark series. The camouflage uniform was printed with a spotty pattern, the shades varying with the season, and it is pointless to try to describe it in words. Use good illustrations, and go slowly. One tip—decide in advance which colours you will use in which order, and stick to it. The SS camouflage features spots of one colour on slightly larger spots of others. It is obviously much easier to blob on the base colour, then a smaller spot of the top shade, rather than trying to outline the inner colour with the outer. The harness and magazine pouches should be black leather, as should the entrenching tool carrier. The poncho is in the same camouflage as the uniform; for the rest, follow the Afrika Korps instructions—shades of greenish-grey, tending to fawn in places, such as on the canteen cover.

The cap should be field-grey. With a thin matt black line, suggest the edge of the 'turn-up'. The skull and eagle are silver-grey on a black backing—paint all over black first, then pick out in silver-grey, leaving a black outline as thin as possible. If you want him to be

Rear view of fully-equipped SS troop-er—note camou-flaged cover on helmet slung above the entrenching tool. The effect of a camouflage cloth can be heightened by putting in seams with faint matt black lines. Note green-on-black Scharführer's *arm rank patch.*

Simpler conversions

an NCO, add the green-bars-on-black rank patch to the left arm, using your reference books for details. Remember to leave small areas unpainted where the helmet is to be slung, in the palm of his right hand to accept the gun, in the palm of his left where it touches the scenery, and on his boot soles.

For scenery we used mainly bits from the useful Tamiya brick wall set, on the base of an Airfix mounted figure. We cut the wall about a bit, roughening its rather too neat outline; we also chopped up one whole segment into individual bricks, for scattered rubble. This, we may add, is the devil's own job — the plastic is incredibly tough, and it took a hacksaw to do the job. *Do not try it with a razor-knife* — you will certainly break the blade and may have a nasty accident. We coated part of the wall with thinly-scraped putty, to stimulate plaster, and added some wood scraps from a cannibalised pencil. A parting thought: urban rubble is more subtly coloured and arranged than you think. Guess at it, and the result will disappoint you. Go to a demolition site — almost everyone lives within reach of one these days, Heaven knows — and look carefully, and take notes. And a parting-parting

thought! We note, for no reason we can see, that the plastic transparency holding the parts of the Coldstream Guards kit we bought at about this time was of very thick, rigid material. Cut carefully at an angle, so as to give a 'chamfered' edge which catches the light, this material makes convincing broken window glass in this scale.

Leutnant, German Infantry, 1944

After making our *Waffen-SS* conversion we decided that the Army should be represented as well. They wore a different camouflage uniform, which also looks attractive in this scale and is rather easier to paint. After considering the bits and pieces in the spares and accessories trays we became fired with enthusiasm for the idea of producing a bazooka crewman, lying in wait for his breakfast Sherman in the Normandy *bocage*. Fortunately we had a bit of scrap plastic base from a plastic palm tree, which was about the right size and irregular shape, so we selected the lying figure of the MG34 gunner from the Afrika Korps Multipose set as the basis for our soldier.

The legs (no 20) and torso (no 17) present no problems and can be cemented together after trimming off the pocket pleats. After experimenting without cement, we decided to trim down quite severely the tail of the jacket where it lies on the right buttock—otherwise the field assault equipment is going to stick up in a most unrealistic fashion. We took head no 16, and after playing around with the other parts for a bit came to the conclusion that a realistic pose required

Completed but unpainted figure of Wehrmacht 'bazooka' operator, with helmet built up with putty and 'soup' to suggest camouflage cover.

us to turn the head half-left, so he would be looking roughly in the same direction as his bazooka. We accordingly trimmed away at the side of the neck, constantly offering it up to the neck of the torso to check fit, until it would sit at the right angle. We then cemented it in place. This inevitably left some visible gaps at the bottom of the join, so we gave him a scarf, using sparingly-applied blobs of plastic 'soup'—but putty can equally well be used.

Next we added arm no 19, and left him to set while assembling the bazooka. This is the beautiful little Panzerschreck from Armour Accessories Set 2, an absolute symphony of delicate, flash-free little struts and sights and handles! It is in 1:35 scale, and thus officially too small for our 54mm or 1:32 soldier; but in fact comparison of the actual dimensions

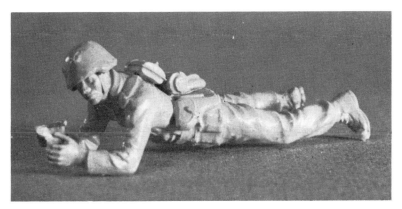

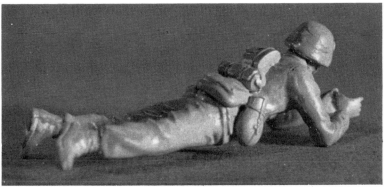

convinces us that it is permissible, if we assume our *leutnant* is a tall man. (The length of the actual weapon was 5 feet 4½ inches, the bore 3½ inches.) Liquid cement is virtually essential in assembling these delicate mouldings. Don't forget to cut from the sprue the projectile, at the same time. It can lie beside our hero, if he is alone on his base; or, if you feel like doing a two-man crew as was more usual, you could have a similarly-dressed trooper crouching behind him holding it—the details are up to your ingenuity!

While the Panzerschreck was drying—we allowed plenty of time, as minimal cement was used—we turned to his helmet. It must have a cloth camouflage cover. We were not entirely satisfied with the attempt at this effect on our *Waffen-SS* man using only blobs of plastic 'soup', so this time we used putty first to get the right general outline, filling in the dip between brim and crown-shoulder like stretched cloth. When it was dry, we returned to it at another convenient moment and filed carefully to the required outline. We finished it off with a 'skin' of plastic soup brushed thinly, and 'tagged' in one or two places just before drying, to give a wrinkled and torn effect. We were much more satisfied with the finished result. At a suitable moment we stuck it on the soldier's head and added a chinstrap from thin plastic card.

We added arm no 29 to the torso, and let it dry thoroughly. We then offered up the Panzerschreck, fitting it into the right hand at a realistic angle, and found—as suspected—that the angle of the left arm must be altered to allow the hand to grasp the front of the trigger frame. With the delightfully 'cheesy' plastic used in these mouldings, such chores are made easy. Carve patiently at the crook of the elbow with a sharp blade, until the arm can be bent into position and held while a blob of cement in the cut dries. Any cosmetic work necessary after drying is the labour of a moment, thanks to 'soup'.

Laying aside the bazooka for painting separately, we added the field equipment. Bread-bag, rolled poncho, mess-tin, and, if you like, an entrenching tool can be added as per the Afrika Korps kit instructions. We wanted our man to be an officer, so put a holster on his belt instead of an entrenching tool and bayonet, and let the canteen hang realistically down on his right side to balance it. The reason for selecting this rank is conscience! The Army rank and file were usually issued with a baggy collarless camouflage smock similar in cut to the earlier SS pattern but in Army pattern material. The four-pocket camouflage jacket, virtually identical in cut to the officer's service tunic, was almost invariably worn by officers.

The best painting reference available at a reasonable price is one of the colour figures (F3) in the Men-at-Arms book *The Panzer Divisions,* though this illustrates an officer of 'Grossdeutschland' with various unauthorised and unit insignia. No badges were supposed to be worn on the camouflage uniform, although collar bars and breast eagles were not unknown. We went by the book, and limited insignia to the rank patch on the left upper arm; this was exactly like the Waffen-SS one for equivalent rank—an oak spray above a bar, both in green, on a black patch.

Rear view of completed model, with figure and Panzerschreck assembled to scenic base. Note camouflage pattern.

Side view of painted model — the green oakleaf-above-bar rank patch on a black backing is just visible on the left upper arm.

(See Figure D1 in the above-mentioned book for an example of these patches.) Note that on the trousers, the camouflage pattern does not continue all the way round. The pattern breaks noticeably at the outside leg seam. The equipment should be in shades of groy-green (bread-bag, canteen cover, mess-tin) and black leather (belt, braces, boots, holster), the poncho in camouflage material. The Panzerschreck should be sand yellow with soft 'sprayed' streaks of dark green in irregular patterns; its projectile should be dirty black.

The base we built up at odd moments during the making of the figure, using putty on the plastic base. We built up a slope for him to lie on, and at one point, while the putty was tacky, wetted the unpainted figure with water and pressed him lightly into the putty at the required angle. The water prevents him picking up putty on his body; the impression remains and hardens, ensuring that he fits properly after painting. We stuck sisal string 'grass', fine gravel, small rocks, and flock into the putty. If you like the general idea of this conversion, but don't wish to go to the trouble and expense of finding a Panzerschreck, then very much the same sequence and parts can be used to give an officer looking through field glasses; or simply peering through the grass with his MP40 in his hand and pouches on his belt; or an MG34 gunner — the MG42 had generally supplanted it by 1944 but it was still to be seen; or even a plain rifleman, with Mauser K98 in hand and stick-grenades lying ready at his elbow.

Simpler conversions

four

Harder conversions

The projects suggested in the previous chapter involved a good deal of mixing-and-matching between parts of the same range of kits, and the occasional fairly radical alteration of a piece by scraping or filing away large areas of surface, or changing its outline in some way. In this chapter we describe four rather more challenging conversions. They involve fitting together parts of different kits, which don't fit without careful modification; quite extensive filling and filing, to marry up the torso from one range with the pelvis from another; and a certain amount of improvisation and scratch-building of minor items.

Private, British Line Infantry, 1815

Modellers wishing to produce small dioramas of Waterloo and Quatre Bras

scenes with the several suitable Airfix figures now available will doubtless have a need for British Guards and infantry figures in positions other than those provided. The famous British square formation involved men kneeling in the front rank, men crouching forward in the second rank, and men standing to fire and reload in the third and fourth ranks. The basic steps of the following conversion can be used, or modified according to individual taste, in a number of ways and for a number of subjects. Our model is of a front-rank private in flank company (grenadier or light) of a line battalion at Waterloo.

Take kits of the 95th Rifleman and 42nd Highlander, and the head and shako from a Coldstream Guards kit. Select the kneeling legs from a Rifle kit, and cement them, performing the usual chores of trimming and filing when set. Take the two halves of the 42nd Highlander torso; on offering it up to the legs, it will be found to be a bit too large at the waist. Trim or file off the slight protruding ridge at the bottom line of the front torso. With a sharp knife, carefully cut away the flat piece of horizontal plastic which closes off the 'stomach'. Trim away the thickness of the front torso at the bottom, to allow the 'pelvis' of the Rifle legs to slip a little way up inside the torso when

Front and rear of complete but unpainted figure of flank company private of British infantry, 1815—note covered shako effect, and base being built up from putty, small stones and sand.

The painted model; facing colour and regimental details are naturally optional. The whole of Wellington's Waterloo infantry could be modelled from kit parts already available in the Airfix range—including foreign troops such as the Hanoverian Landwher!

offered up, so that the front bottom line of the jacket does not stick forward from the 'stomach' too proud. Trim and file until the result looks right; then join the two halves of the torso, and join torso to pelvis. Allow plenty of time to dry, and handle with care—this will not make a very strong joint. At the moment of sticking, make sure the shoulders are at the proper angle to ground level, and not slanting one way or the other. When dry, you may have to do a little filling here and there to fair the two halves of the body together, and to build out the stomach a little below the jacket, using putty or careful applications of plastic 'soup'.

Take a Coldstream head, and cut off the neck. It is too thick for the collar hole in the Black Watch torso, and the shako does not fit well on the Black Watch head. Taking care not to allow cement spillage, glue the neckless head into the top of the collar. Cement the Coldstream shako in place, but do not add cords, plume or badge. The idea is to try to simulate the wrapped shako in its oilcloth waterproof cover, as this was certainly worn at Waterloo by most redcoats. If you wish you can make the slightly bulging, horizontally creased outline with carefully applied 'strings' of putty, coating the whole, when dry, with several thick layers of

'soup'—or, as in our model, you can use 'soup' alone. Go slowly, and make sure the folds are all horizontal rather than vertical—you can use the consistency of the 'soup', and gravity, to achieve this, by turning the shako gently and allowing drops to run around it. As always, the watchword is 'slow and careful'. Make sure the 'soup' does not drip on to the face. You could also set in the front, low down, a little knot of tied thread.

When this operation is completed, you can add the equipment. This should be exactly as per the 42nd Highlander kit instructions. You can use the Highlander's belt plate at the junction of the crossbelts on the chest, on the upper (bayonet) crossbelt. When on the field of battle troops tended to remove and pile their knapsacks, so only crossbelts with pouch and bayonet, haversack and canteen should be worn. When these are set, with straps crossing shoulders close to the neck but not touching it, you can add the arms. Use 42nd Highlander right arm, no 28, set on the shoulder at such an angle that the thumb just touches the outside of the thigh. Use the Highlander's left arm no 25. Your model is now complete except for shoulder straps and musket. We used flank company wings from the

Highlander kit, but a centre company man can be made simply by substituting the straps with tufted ends from the same kit. The musket should be fitted with a fixed bayonet, as in the kit instructions.

Consult your reference library for colours. The singly spaced bastion-shaped lace loops on the chest will limit the choice of purists to three Waterloo regiments—the 2nd Battalion/30th Foot, Cambridgeshire Regiment, which had yellow facings and silver metal; the 2nd Battalion/73rd Foot, Highland Regiment, which had green facings and gold metal; and the 1st Battalion/4th Foot, King's Own Regiment, which had blue facings and gold metal. The first two served in Halkett's Brigade of Alten's 3rd British Division, one of the most heavily engaged of all Waterloo formations; the last served with Lambert's Brigade of the 6th British Division. The shako cover should be painted glossy or semi-gloss black, using horizontal brush-strokes. The dull red tunic has facings on collar, shoulder straps, and cuffs, and white lace in this scale. Note that unlike the Guards, flank companies of line regiments had *red* shoulder wings, laced and tufted white.

The model can be realistically posed on a landscape base of grass, mud, or even cornstalks made from sisal string. A discarded Cuirassier helmet from the relevant kit will make a nice 'prop', lying at our redcoat's feet.

Rifleman, 60th Rifles, 1808-15

Hamilton Smith's famous series of uniform engravings, now reproduced by the National Army Museum as coloured postcards, are one of our primary sources of information on British Napoleonic soldiers. That devoted to the Rifles, illustrated in black and white here, features a kneeling soldier of the 95th with, standing priming his rifle in the background, a man of the 60th Regiment. This large corps had several red-coated battalions and two green-jacketed rifle battalions, of which the most famous was the 5th/60th. Some

Hamilton Smith's famous study of 60th and 95th Riflemen inspired the 60th Rifles conversion, a fairly easy modification of the Airfix kit.

of the personnel were a shade colourful by normal Line standards, being odds and ends of foreign volunteer units, and even at times 'turned around' enemy prisoners. Nevertheless, the battalion proved itself again and again in the Peninsula campaigns as a crack unit of unquestionable loyalty. Its strength was usually dispersed, individual companies being assigned to brigades and divisions of infantry throughout the army to strengthen their skirmishing line. It occured to us that it might be attractive to prepare a conversion of one of these characters, as near to the pose of the Hamilton Smith picture as possible, so that modellers could combine it with a kneeling 95th Rifleman straight from the Airfix kit in a three-dimensional version of the picture. On a suitable base, in front of a coloured postcard of the picture from the NAM in a small frame, it would make an attractive little display.

You will need a 95th Rifleman and a Black Watch kit, with an Afrika Korps arm and the cords from a Coldstream shako or from Historex spares. First, the legs. Take the Rifleman's standing legs, and with the picture in front of you cut them off with a razor-saw at the level of the top of the short gaiters. It is best

Undercoated model of 60th Rifleman; the Baker rifle will be added after painting is complete.

Note powder-horn cord passing through paper 'tube' on crossbelt, and extra cords added to rear of shako.

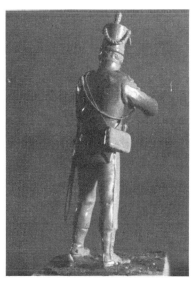

to cement them together at this stage, and when set firmly, to trim and file moulding lines and to file the edges of the raw 'stumps' inward, to stimulate trousers tucked into gaiter-tops. Note, however, that you *should not trim off* the prominent welt down the outside legs for this model. Next, take the Rifleman's torso, and cement it together. When dry, trim off the two vertical lines of lace on the back of the jacket, and the rear pair of buttons (the lace, because it is not thought to have appeared on the 60th jacket, and the buttons, so that the waist-belt can lie flat). Trim off the bottom trio of front buttons for the same reason. The turnbacks are too thick, and must be patiently filed down into a more natural appearance, hardly standing proud of the jacket. When torso trimming is complete, stick it to the legs.

Take 42nd Highlander legs, and carefully saw off the feet and ankles, on a line level with the top front line of the gaiters. The cut should be straight, leaving the rear point of the gaiter on the discarded legs. (If you have them in the spares box, you could use several other legs for this—French 1815 line infantryman, British Grenadier 1776, American infantryman 1776, or French Imperial Guard Grenadier—in fact any figure with gaiters up to mid-calf or higher.) Be sure to offer up the legs from which you are going to cut the feet, and the Rifleman's legs, and mark the exact line with the edge of a blade before beginning sawing—otherwise you may wind up with a Rifleman with ludicrously long or short or, worse, uneven legs! File the ends of your amputated gaitered ankles clean, checking fit and angle against the leg stumps, then cement in place and leave well alone until properly set. When dry, the new legs can be filled, or trimmed to reinforce the impression of trousers tucked into gaiters.

Next, cement the Rifleman's head to the torso. Take the Rifleman's shako, and with a sharp blade and files, carefully remove the cord detail moulded to it. Do *not* accidentally cut off the tufts; take your time. When this is done, cement peak to shako, shako to head, and cockade and bugle-horn badge to shako. Leave to dry; then add cords from a Coldstream shako, or trimmed and bent from the lengths supplied on some Historex headgear sprues, using the Hamilton Smith picture as a guide. Note that the picture clearly suggests that the cords, hooked to the top edge of the shako at right and left, then continued right round the back of the shako. We had the luck of finding a second set of Coldstream cords in the spares box, left over from previous conversions with covered shakos, so trimmed the bunch of tassels from one end and bent the cord to shape, cementing it in place butting against the ends of the front cords. Cords need not lie absolutely flat to the shako, but can 'fly' a little, adding to the lifelike quality of the figure.

We decided to add the left arm at this stage, then the equipment, and finally the bent right arm, which would otherwise have made fitting the bandolier difficult. We used the left arm of a Black Watch figure, at the high port, to support the Baker rifle while priming. Remember to trim cuff detail off before adding the arm—the cuff will have to be painted in a pointed shape. Then we added the waist-belt, buckle, bayonet and frog, bullet pouch, bandolier and cartridge pouch exactly as per the 95th kit instructions. We left off the pack, haversack and canteen, in accordance with the Hamilton Smith picture, but if you are not consciously trying to copy it then haversack and canteen, pushed well back behind the left hip, would be realistic. When all this was dry we added the right arm; no 23 from the Afrika Korps Multipose kit is perfect. The Baker was trimmed and laid aside ready for painting and adding at the last minute, after the figure had been painted.

The last step occurred to us on the spur of the moment—it worked, and you may like to try it, as it gives a pleasing effect even if rather out of scale. The cord on which the powder-horn was slung lay not just over the bandolier, but actually attached to it—it passed through some tiny loops or tubes of

Front of painted figure, with rifle inserted into left hand.

leather attached to the face of the bandolier. We succeeded in simulating this effect by taking tiny strips of thin paper and rolling them round a pin. The tubes thus formed were cut off with a razor-knife and cemented to the bandolier with liquid cement, one on the chest and one in the small of the back. Liquid cement should hold them without filling them up. We then threaded nylon thread used for the horn cord through the tubes, leaving plenty of slack hanging at each end. The horn was cemented into the right hand, and the threads brought up and glued to the ends of the horn, the surplus being cut off after drying. After all this was dry we cemented the shoulder straps in place, using the centre-company tufted straps from the Highlander kit. The model is now finished, apart from

Rear of figure; there is still uncertainty abour rear coatee detail in this unit, so we stuck to plain red turnbacks and no lace.

adding the rifle and its sling after painting.

Paint the figure largely as in the Hamilton Smith painting. The shako is black, with green tuft and cords, silver button, black cockade and silver badge. The jacket is Rifle green with silver buttons, and unpiped red collar, pointed cuffs, shoulder straps and tufts. The turnbacks are variously shown as either solid red, or green piped red at the edge—take your choice. The overalls are dark blue with a red welt down the outside, the gaiters dark grey, and all equipment exactly as in the 95th kit instructions. The moustache was sometimes worn by German soldiers in British service, and many served in the 5th/60th; the chin-strap of the shako, shown by Hamilton Smith, is also optional.

Lieutenant, RTR, 1941

The Airfix 8th Army Multipose kit, with its original headgear, offers the possibility not only of infantry figures but also of tank crewmen. With the Airfix 1:32 scale Crusader tank kit available, the modeller can easily produce a varied group of crew figures for the kind of 'moment of leisure' dioramas which allow scope for individual imagination. We decided to make a tank commander figure to typify the style of the old desert hands, immortalised in the wartime cartoons of Jon's 'Two Types'. He is a Second Lieutenant of the Royal Tank Regiment.

We took a pair of Coldstream Guardsman legs from the spares box and trimmed off the outside welts and the moulding lines; the front 'fall' was also filed away, and a couple of slit pockets scribed in the outside of the thighs. Gaiter detail was cut from the boots, and the little triangular cut-outs at the outside of each ankle were filled with putty. We selected a torso from the 8th Army kit; preferably, use one which is slightly higher at the front than at the back, as the waist surface of the lower half of the body slopes backwards slightly. We filed a smooth surface on the top of the leg assembly, and cemented the torso to it. We then added 8th Army head no 21, and beret no 63, after cleaning the moulding lines from both with a sharp blade.

When the joints are dry, fill the slightly undercut waist area with putty. We took the opportunity of adding at this point a neckerchief, also from putty; and a suitably aggressive moustache, from tiny blobs of putty applied on the tip of the knife. When the waist filling was dry we filed it smooth, then coated both it and the scarf with a layer of 'soup'. We worked on the separate pieces of equipment until this coating was dry, then added the arms—8th Army nos 19 or 24 for the left, and no 13 for the right. The joints were trimmed and coated with 'soup' when the cement was firm.

The 8th Army web holster could be used straight from the kit if preferred, but we decided on something more ambitious and attractive. The low-slung open-top holster issued to tank crews is illustrated here in the photos; you can also see it as Fig 62 of Mollo and McGregor's *Army Uniforms of World War 2* by Blandford. We cut the top section from the web holster, and mounted the rest on a strap made from plastic card, about 10mm long by 3mm wide. This passed under the web belt, the tapered end passing down again and into a buckle in front. A false tongue-and-buckle section was made from plastic card and a tiny Historex buckle, and cemented flat on the main strap. We cut a revolver from the 8th Army kit in two at the correct point, just in front of the hammer, and cemented it to the top of the holster. The retaining strap was made from plastic card, as was the long, narrow vertical pocket on the front of the holster which held the cleaning rod; this latter was made from a single strand of copper wire stripped out of an old piece of electric flex, the loop at the top formed round a rat-tail file. The line of six spare cartridges could be made from thin stretched sprue, but we had a

Model kit manufacturers nearly always provide at least a commander figure with tank kits nowadays; but even so, modellers of AFVs would do well to consider conversions in this area. 'Ready-made' tank commanders tend to be of variable quality, and rather stiff in appearance—with the notable exception of some recent productions by Tamiya. The figures in the hatches of this 7th Royal Tank Regiment Matilda II are modifications of Tamiya figures, and add a good deal to the appeal of the model. The RTR sergeant clambering from his turret wears battledress blouse and khaki drill slacks, a not unusual combination in the desert.

Above left *Completed RTR officer model, set on base and undercoated. Note detail of armoured troops' leg-mounted holster; cigarette packet; and Historex mug in right hand.* **Centre** *Another angle of the tank commander model, showing to advantage the facial character imparted by the new moustache and cigarette.* **Right** *The RTR figure at an early stage of painting. Some basic areas of colour have been laid down, and a start made on the eyes.*

section of 1:35 scale machine-gun belt from Armour Accessories Set No 4, and made ours by trimming off six rounds and cutting them in half.

I he holster was strapped to the right thigh, so we made a leg-strap from a strip of 2mm plastic card and cemented it in place with a 'tail' protruding outwards behind the leg. A buckle was made from an Airfix Polish Lancer's carbine swivel and cemented on the strap behind the leg. The cartridge pouch is simple to make from one of the rifle pouches in the 8th Army kit. Cut off the top 3mm of this, and file the back until it is about half the original thickness. Round off the corners with a file, and remove the fastening strap from the edge of the flap downwards — the pistol pouch closed with a press-stud. Cement the pouch to a square of plastic card very slightly larger than itself, so a narrow edge shows all round; then cement it to the left front of the belt.

To be honest, when we began this conversion we had in mind that our

'Skipper' should hold a compass in his raised left hand, as if just taking a sighting, and a folded map in the right hand. Something about the pose of the almost completed figure caught our imagination, however; we decided to have him taking a break for char and a smoke, and offering his cigarettes to a friend. The mug in the right hand came from a Historex sprue of pots and pans, invaluable for the conversion maniac! The pack of cigarettes was made from scrap plastic, its open flap from scored plastic card, and the cigarettes themselves from (since they were still sculling around the modelling bench) the trimmed off halves of the cartridges which went on his holster! Stretched sprue would do just as well.

When everything was set we had a final session with 'soup', covering any fine cracks and ensuring that the filled areas were smooth. We also put a blob on his beret at this point, for a badge — you could simply paint it on, but it looks better standing slightly proud. We painted his shirt pale drill,

Harder conversions

his webbing yellowish khaki with bronze buckles and tags, his gun-butt and cleaning rod black, his beret matt black with a silver badge, and his mug white with tiny blue 'chipped enamel' areas on the rim. The scarf can be any pattern you like. The boots can be black or brown leather, or painted to resemble suede chukka boots. The slacks can be ordinary pale drill, or, if you have the patience, you could paint a multitude of very fine vertical lines to simulate the corduroy popular with some officers in the desert. Posed on the decking of a Crusader, say, offering a smoke to another commander sitting in the open hatch, this dashing warrior adds a nice touch of authentic casualness to any model. He doesn't *have* to be an officer, of course; with drill slacks, he could equally well be an NCO or trooper, but we felt the moustache had an unmistakably commissioned air. His pips would take the form of tiny diamonds of red on the shoulder-straps, with a white blob in the centre of each. Optional extras could include a pistol lanyard of khaki thread, from the butt to either the neck or the shoulder; binoculars; or goggles on the beret.

Captain, British Infantry, 1776

As soon as we saw it we were struck by the conversion possibilities of the Airfix mounted kit of George Washington. Since War of Independence figures are very much in vogue at the moment, we decided to make up an officer of the British Line in the unlaced coat often worn when in the field during that war, using parts of the Washington and Continental infantryman kits with Historex legs.

The main idea was to utilise the coat of the Washington figure, which is of typical cut for the period, and which also has its tails 'flying'—pushed up by the rump of the horse in this mounted kit. Use this coat on a running figure, and you have a nice impression of movement and action suitable for an officer leading his men in a charge.

We took the excellently moulded head and tricorne hat from the American Continental infantryman kit and used them without alteration. The entire George Washington torso and

Undercoated figure of running 18th Century British officer, from George Washington and Historex parts.

Study photos of actual garments, or better still, visit museums and see the real thing. In the 'flesh', you can often spot surprising details about the clothes of previous centuries which you might never have suspected, and this background information can only benefit your modelling. This is the coat of Captain Thomas Plumbe, an officer of the Royal Lancashire Militia in about 1760; it is red, as are the vest and breeches, with blue facings and gold lace, including the single epaulette on the right shoulder. Note its characteristic flat outline.

arms can be used with very little change. An epaulette must be added to the right shoulder. We used one from the spares box, originally part of the Airfix 1815 Imperial Guard Grenadier kit. File away the incorrect button from the outer end, and cut the strap off diagonally so that it gives the impression of passing under the falling collar of the coat. Notch the fringe with a sharp blade, to give it more life and movement, and cement it in place on the torso after you have completed the usual operations of joining front and back halves and arms and working over the joint-line. Washington wears the

Harder conversions

ribbon of an order across his chest under the coat. It is a simple matter to file this flat, so that it resembles a sword baldric passing under the coat, and to add a rectangular 'plate' from plastic card on the exposed section.

The arms are in a convincing position for a man running, his left arm working back and forth to keep his balance, with a sword in his right hand. Legs, however, cannot be found in exactly the position we wanted, so we had to work on a pair of Historex French Heavy Cavalry legs from their spares

The British Grenadier and American Soldier 1775 kits in the Airfix range suggest many possible conversions of the Seven Years' and French-Indian Wars. This is the typical cut and decoration of a British infantryman's coat of the 1750s. Of coarse brick-red cloth, it was fully lined and faced with the regimental facing colour, and laced with white tape bearing the coloured line pattern peculiar to that regiment. The skirts were usually worn hooked up, and the lapels could be buttoned across the chest in foul weather.

Model Soldiers

list. The left leg was re-positioned so that it took up the 'trailing' stance of a running man, the foot just leaving the ground. You will have to do a good deal of filing, offering up, and filing once again before you can marry the two legs at the thigh at the right angle and with the right dimensions. The joining of the Airfix torso and Historex legs at the waist also takes a good deal of careful work, carving and filing. Try to find a suitable photograph of a man — any man — running in this position, so that you can ensure the correct angle; note that the body leans well forward of the vertical.

British officers wore a waist sash of crimson knotted over the vest but under the coat, with generously fringed

Two of the many kinds of 'Light Infantry cap' worn in the 1770s and 1780s by British Army skirmishers. Some were made specially from felt or leather, but the majority seem to have been cut down with some ingenuity from issue tricorne hats. Fur, feathers, cow-tails, and other kinds of decorations were common.

Partially completed conversion of the Airfix Grenadier kit into a man of a battalion company. This and other variations were described in detail in Airfix Magazine of April 1976.

Harder conversions

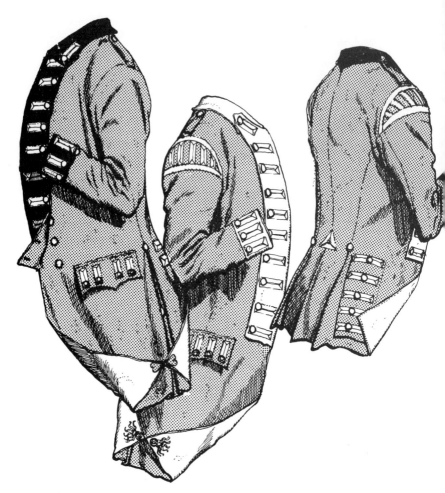

hanging tassels on the left hip. Sashes can be simulated by a smear of putty, which can be worked with a dampened blade while still tacky; give it hard edges top and bottom, and a creased surface appearance. The tassels we used were cut from the flag in the American 1776 infantryman kit. (This flag is far too small and should not be used for the purpose for which it is supplied; it is a useful source of spares, however.) We cut them off just above the head of the tassel and cemented them on the left hip just under the edge of the open coat, in a realistic 'bouncing' position. We took the slim

Coats of privates of the British Infantry of the late 18th Century; the plain coat of the battalion companies, the grenadier's coat with its shoulder 'wings', and the cut-down coat of the light infantry companies. There were many variations of the latter, but the example illustrated is fairly typical.

sword-scabbard from the same kit, and pushed the top of it up under the coat, cementing it behind the tassels so that the scabbard appeared to be frogged to the almost-hidden baldric and flying

Model Soldiers

up with the motion of running. The sword was cemented in the right hand. Structurally, the model is now complete, apart from a little fist-strap with a tasselled end for the sword, made from card.

Since this is the unlaced coat worn in the field, you can paint it up as of any regiment you wish. Reference can be found in Osprey's Men-at-Arms series, *The British Army in North America, 1775-83*, by Robin May, illustrated by Gerry Embleton. We selected a regiment with blue facings and silver metal, the 4th (King's Own) Foot. The coat is bright scarlet, with dark blue collar, lapels, and cuffs. The turn backs are white, as is the visible lining of the coat on the underside of the tails. The vest and breeches, baldric, and lace at throat and cuff are all white. The stock is black, as are the boots—the latter being of a type typically worn by officers when they spent most of their time in the saddle, infantry or not. The hat is black with a matt finish, the scabbard semi-gloss black like the boots. The cockade is gloss black, fixed by a silver loop and button. All the buttons are silver, as is the epaulette, the belt-plate, the hilt of the sword, and the lacing round the edge of the hat. The spurs are steel; the hair should be painted natural colour, bound with a black ribbon. The fist-strap is gold and crimson mixed, the sword blade bright silver.

When selecting your subject for this model, remember that not all British regiments wore white small-clothes and equipment. Some had buff vest, breeches, turnbacks, lining, and leather belts. Check your references before starting to paint the uniform. A very good introduction to the subject by Bryan Fosten, appeared in *Airfix Magazine Annual 5*.

The same structural conversion can be used, with the omission of the sash, for an American officer, in a dark blue coat lined white and faced in the colour of his state's line, and white small-clothes. An exact subject can be selected from the Blandford book by Mollo and McGregor, *Uniforms of the American Revolution*.

five

Flexing
your muscles

In this final chapter, we describe three conversions which call for extensive scratch-building; the almost complete alteration of major parts, picked for little more than their basic identity as limbs and trunks; and a great deal of careful and imaginative work with putty, card and liquid plastic 'soup'. We hope that they will inspire modellers who have got this far, not to copy them slavishly, but to work out their own variations on the same techniques and to create models which reflect their own particular enthusiasms.

Piper, Seaforth Highlanders, 1942

This is quite a challenging conversion, as it involves both the matching of moulded parts from different kits, and a certain amount of scratch-building; the final paint job is also rather demanding, so all in all it makes a good subject for our chapter of progressively more complex projects. It makes a most attractive single model; or you could use it in a small diorama with other Airfix Multipose 8th Army figures, depicting a squad on the march or advancing in North Africa. Those modellers who now feel like tackling quite a large diorama could combine it with an Airfix 1:32 scale Crusader and some crew figures (see chapter 4) in an El Alamein scene.

You will need an 8th Army kit, a Waterloo 42nd Highlander kit, various bits and pieces from the spares box, and, for reference, Robin Adair's *British 8th Army, North Africa, 1940-43* in the Key Uniform Guide series—at 95p a most

useful source of inspiration for all 8th Army conversions. The piper model was suggested to us by a photo—fig 25 in Adair's book—of a Cameron Highlanders piper. We chose to make a Seaforth because another photo—fig 41—shows good insignia detail, and because the Seaforth tartan is a little less terrifying when it comes to painting the kilt! There were two battalions of Seaforths with 51st Highland Division at El Alamein.

Assemble the halves of the kilt from the Black Watch kit, trimming off the two small rear pegs. Take 8th Army kit torso no 22, and after trimming add head no 11. Cut a very narrow strip of plastic card from the sheet provided and cement it to the head all round the brows just above the eyes and

Above left *Right side of completed and undercoated piper model. Note angle of legs.* **Centre** *Another angle on the piper, showing small pack slung on left hip, and bag of pipes under left elbow.* **Right.** *On our model the bagpipes are noticeably overscale as regards the thickness of the pipes; since you won't be working to a deadline, presumably you can arrange to avoid this . . . Note linking piece of webbing from under pistol cartridge pouch to front buckle of small pack, added from plastic card; and fish-tail flashes on hose-tops.*

ears — this is to suggest the lining of the steel helmet, which looks too big and empty without it. Cut a chin strap from the same sheet and add it to the head at this stage. Cement torso and kilt together and set aside.

Take 8th Army legs no 5, and saw them carefully apart. Holding the legs vertically, gripping the foot and with the top braced on your modelling table, take a sharp blade and carefully shave the shorts detail right off, trimming the

leg to a thin peg at the top. File the thighs clean when this is complete; you don't have to get a perfect surface as it will be hidden by the kilt. Then, using the Black Watch legs as a guide, cut your new legs to the right length — this means taking about 3/16 inch off the top end of each, but pick your own line after consulting the photo of the piper quoted above; the kilt should come just to the top of the kneecap. Insert the legs in the kilt to check length and fit, and when satisfied, cement in place. When the cement has dried, it's a good idea to drip generous blobs of 'soup' up into the kilt, to flow around the tops of the legs and form a firm joint when dry. Obviously, allow this to dry with the figure standing upside-down.

At this point we added the personal equipment. The web pistol holster from the 8th Army kit goes on the right front of the belt; the water-bottle fits on the right hip with its left hand slinging strap joined by a tiny strip of plastic card to the right rear belt buckle, and its right hand slinging strap disappearing up behind the holster. A small pack is worn on the left hip, united by small strips of plastic card to the left rear belt buckle, and the attachment point of the left shoulder brace and the belt at the front. Leave a little 'tail' of strap hanging down each end face of the small pack below the cementing point; and cover the cementing points with a couple of tiny buckles from the spares box—we used Historex musket sling buckles. The only other equipment worn is the pistol cartridge pouch, which is clearly illustrated in the Key Uniform Guide book, both in photos and in colour on the inside back cover. It is simple to make by cutting one of the rifle cartridge pouches from the 8th Army kit in two, and filing the top half thinner before mounting it on a little square of plastic card and sticking it to the left front of the belt. We took this opportunity to add the fish-tail garter flashes to the outside of each sock; you could cut down the more elaborate flashes from the Black Watch kit, but it is quicker to make them from plastic card. We then stuck the figure to a base, and when dry applied the basic ground for the scenic base with putty, building it up around the feet first and then working outwards. The model was left overnight to set firmly.

The arms we used were nos 8 and 9 from the 8th Army kit. They have to stand out from the body more than in the standard figure; we used the photo quoted above of the Cameron piper as our guide here, checking with great care that the hands finished up in the correct positions. We cemented the

arms at the right angle, with liquid cement at the point of contact and in the open gap left between the parts by the new angle. Into this we poked little chips of polystyrene from our shorts-chopping session earlier on, until the gap was roughly filled and the arms had a fairly firm surface to grip on. When the cement was dry we carefully

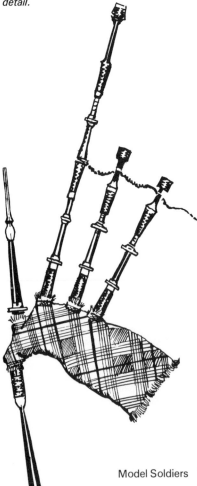

Simplified sketch of a set of bagpipes. If you can't locate a moulded metal set to scale, from some proprietary model figure, then before you are far advanced with scratch-building you may curse the day you were born—but soldier on, the result is worth it! Pipes are ebony, 'collars' and 'muzzles' white; there are many variations of cord and ribbon detail.

Model Soldiers

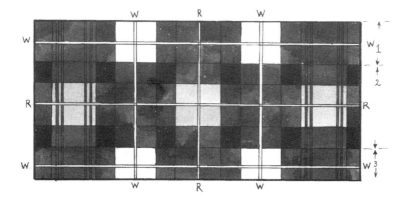

A patch of Seaforth tartan. White squares represent green, lightly shaded squares a smoky dark blue, and all others varying shades produced by black shadowing over green or blue. Rows (1) and (3) are basically green, and row (2) basically blue. The black corner squares are intersections of black-over-blue. R = a red line, W = a white line. In 54mm scale a reasonable approximation of the pattern can be achieved in the following way. Paint the kilt blue all over, then paint a broad grid of dark green over it. Where green lines intersect, paint little squares of lighter green. Outline all lines and squares with narrow matt black lines; finally, paint on the red and white lines, the former intersecting over blue squares, the latter over green squares. The whole exercise is going to be sheer hell, but in this scale an impression of the right sett is all you can hope for anyway.

dripped 'soup' into the 'rubble-filled' gaps until the armpit was smooth and full. When the 'soup' was quite firm we carved and filed around the whole joint until the finish was perfect. Do not hurry this step—you can be getting on with the bagpipes while the various stages dry. You can add the steel helmet while the final job is setting—one of the ones without a string net cover. Remember that its angle should parallel that of the card head-band cemented on earlier.

We could no longer avoid the bagpipes, and, gritting our teeth, turned to the spares box and the photo. (We have prepared a simple sketch of this misbegotten offspring of an octopus and a haggis for your guidance—we wish somebody had done the same for us!) Every modeller will study the problem in his own way, but this is the sequence we used: first, we made the rough shape of the bag from Plasticine and forced it under the left arm, carving and pushing and

adding bits until it looked roughly right. Then we very carefully inserted the various pipes—see next paragraph—into the Plasticine at the angles suggested by the photo; and finally we built up the now-distorted bag again with tiny bits of Plasticine applied on a knife-tip. Finally, we coated the Plasticine with several careful layers of 'soup' to give a firm shell for painting and to grip the tips of the pipes.

The pipes have various collars and thick sections around them, as the sketch shows, and large flat disc-shaped ends. How you make them depends on the state of your spares box. We used several bits of suspension and exhaust assembly from an old 1:76 scale Airfix US half-track as the basis. The thicker collars were made by rolling tiny strips of paper round the pipe and coating with liquid cement. The ends of the pipes can be made quite convincingly from wheel-hubs (parts 41, 42, 85-88) from the Airfix 88mm gun tractor. The

Flexing your muscles . . .

decorative cords are thread, and the tassel is from a Historex trumpet accessories sprue.

Painting is straightforward apart from the kilt, pipes, and helmet. Follow kit instructions for shirt, legs, webbing and helmet, but paint a Seaforth badge in white on a black square on the left side of the helmet, as photo 41 in the Key Uniform Guide book — this badge is a crown above an L in between the antlers of a full-face stag's head over a scroll. The pipes should be gloss black with matt white collars, etc, and green cord. The bag is in Seaforth tartan, as is the kilt — see illustration herewith. The garter flashes are khaki. Usually divisional insignia were not worn on the drill shirt, but the 51st Division seem to have worn — sometimes at least — shoulder straps with the insignia at the outer end. If you want to try this, the Key Uniform Guide photo shows it well.

American Volunteer Rifleman, 18th Century

This project, and the next, should be seen rather as indications of methods for experiment by the individual modeller than as detailed 'recipes'. The basic materials and techniques are outlined; but until you try to work with, say, softened plastic card yourself,

The model painted and complete. We are not proud of our efforts at painting tartan, but luckily the human eye is less demanding than the close-up lens.

Helmet badge for Seaforth piper, in white on a black square, about 2½ inches square on the left side of the helmet skull.

there is no point in us laying down rigid lists of parts, sizes, patterns, orders of work, and so on. The basic figure we have modelled represents the ubiquitous backwoodsman, with fringed hunting shirt and long rifle, of all America's early wars from the 1740s to the 1830s. Modellers attracted by the image should find specific reference for the period and area they prefer, and modify our description as they go. Books which may be useful include *Military Dress of North America, 1665-1970,* by the present author and artist, published by Ian Allan; *Wolfe's Army* by Robin May and Gerry Embleton, Osprey Men-at-Arms series; *Uniforms of the American Revolution* by Mollo and McGregor, in the Blandford colour series; and various publications and prints produced over the past year or so in celebration of the American bi-centennial.

Your basic aim is to produce a figure with a loose, bulky torso and arms, and a frock effect round the legs. Since all detail will be covered, any torso will do. Either use one which has plenty of bulk, and carve and file away all detail and much of the surface to produce the required creases; or build putty up over the plastic, and file it when dry. For the basis of our figure we used a Historex torso, married at the waist to the kilt from an Airfix 42nd Highlander. This latter was notched at the bottom front, then covered with thin plastic card pressed well into a thick coat of liquid cement. It melts to the extent that you can 'push' basic creases into the surface, and the edge can be fringed

The baggy arms of this model started life as the kneeling legs from an Airfix 95th Rifleman kit. The figure is largely card and putty, built up on a convenient torso and legs from the spares box. Details of dress and equipment are to individual taste. A pleasing variation might be to fit him with scratch-built snow-shoes, adding winter features like a scarf tying the hat on and big mittens, and setting the model on a snow-covered base.

Flexing your muscles . . .

with a knife. If you carve your basic shape from a putty surface, or from scrap plastic, then strips of card fringing can be added and faired in by applications of 'soup'—which we also used extensively to build up the creased surface all over the model, and to smooth the results of the more brutal carving and filing. The caped shoulder effect was built up with 'soup', the final surface being fringed with faired-in card. The collar was added from plastic card as well; the head can start life as any half-head in the spares box, with putty clubbed hair. The slouch hat was made by sticking a disc of thin card to the half-head, and bending up the brim after slightly softening it with cement; building up a crown from putty applied to a piece of suitably sized scrap, to act as a key; then filing to shape, and coating with 'soup'.

The bulky arms defeated us briefly, but eventually began to take shape under Gerry's scalpel—using a 95th Rifleman's *kneeling legs* as the basis! The main creases were going in the right directions, and the rest was simply a matter of patient carving and filing. Hands came from the spares box, as did the buckle and hatchet. The belts are plastic card, the hunting-knife a cut-down Baker sword-bayonet, and the pouch carved sprue, with a card flap. The legs began life as those of a War of Independence British Grenadier. All surface detail was filed off, and the thighs carved right down to pegs until they fitted up the kilt. The Indian *mitasse* leggings were made by cementing a vertical strip of card down the outside of each leg, standing a little proud (they could equally be fringed), and then coating the whole leg with 'soup' to fair in the fringes and built up a smooth painting surface at the same time. The feet were carved down to represent moccasins. Thongs and cords can be stripped from Historex belting material. The powder-horn, with its tiny hanging powder-measure, was carved from scrap sprue. It is a tiresome shape to file, and 54mm metal castings are available if you prefer. The long rifle was made by joining sections of two spare Baker rifles. Painting is naturally up to the individual, who can select whatever shades of rawhide, homespun, and blanket cloth he likes, and whatever degree of decoration.

Warrior, 6th to 10th Century

Once your mind is open to the possibilities of using kit parts not just as mix-and-match ingredients within the same general period, but as the most basic raw materials for what is virtually scratch-building, then the sky is the limit. The spare arm becomes not just a possible Napoleonic arm with a Polish cuff, but *any* arm in history. As we have seen, the bent leg can equally well become an arm, providing a rough angled shape with major creases moulded in already for anything you wish to make. With knife, files, putty, card and liquid polystyrene, you can let your imagination range freely.

Our final project, illustrated unpainted and without undercoat to emphasise the different materials and the amount of 'freehand' work involved, is an example of a shape which could be finished and decorated as any kind of European warrior of the five centuries preceding the Norman Conquest, and as many kinds of early medieval figure. The basic building-blocks were an Airfix 8th Army torso, a Black Watch kilt, 8th Army legs, and Historex arms and hands. The 8th Army and Afrika Korps Multipose sets provide several marvellously expressive heads, whose completeness (as opposed to the normal kit head, which might be described as a 'water-line model'!) allows the building up of many kinds of helmet or cap without difficulty.

The torso had all surface detail such as straps and collar trimmed away, and the mutilated areas were then coated with putty. When dry this was filed and carved into continuations of the moulded creases which remained, and shaped to give more bag at the waist. The kilt was sandpapered at the front and coated with putty at the back, to destroy some of the checked effect and the too-neat pleats. All this putty work can be painted with plastic 'soup' to provide a smooth painting surface later on. The 8th Army legs were severely

Almost any type of warrior of the Dark Ages or early medieval period can be modelled by these basic techniques. Different weapons can be carved from Napoleonic pioneer tools, spontoons and sword-bayonets.

The 'flying cloak' effect, built up by applying layer after layer of plastic 'soup' to a Plasticine former which is removed when the liquid has set firmly.

carved about the thighs until they fitted into the kilt. The boot detail was carved a bit, to give a slimmer shape — remember that shoes of this period were more like moccasins than any modern shoe with an applied sole. The

surface of the hose and puttees was filed and carved to work in more random creases; at a later stage this can be painted with 'soup' to give an effect of rumpled leggings — cross-gartering could also be added from strips of card or Historex belting.

An Afrika Korps head was cemented in place, then given a coating of putty. This was built up on the skull, and worked into 'hair' round the sides and back. When dry, the skull was filed into a smooth, regular cone. Narrow strips of plastic card were pre-bent and cemented in a cruciform frame over the skull, with a long protruding nasal bar at the front; a thicker strip round the brows finishes the head off nicely. This type of helmet was widely used for centuries, either with metal panels or simply a stiff leather cap inside an iron strap frame.

The belts were made from card, of course; and the waistbelt was given a decorative Celtic-type buckle — hidden by the shield in the photos — from a 95th Rifleman's shako cockade. The small sword is carved down from a Baker sword-bayonet, the spear from the American War of Independence spontoon. The shield was cut from an Airfix stand, and filed to shape. A hole was drilled in the centre, and a counter-sunk hand-grip was fitted from sprue; the hole was then covered with a boss cut from an old aircraft propeller spinner. The surface of a shield can be treated as you like — scored for simple planking, roughened for old hide, studded with shavings from sprue or plastic rod, or left smooth for intricate painting.

The flying cloak is an attractive feature of this model, and was made in a way which can be applied with equal success to a wide variety of 'blowing cloth' effects. The method might be called the 'Embleton Lost-Plasticine Process'! A lump of Plasticine was pressed to the shoulders and worked round the neck; then the *upper* surface was carefully shaped and carved into suitable wrinkles and creases. When Gerry was satisfied with the result, he began an endlessly-repeated process of painting this Plasticine surface with

Flexing your muscles . . .

plastic 'soup'. Coat after coat was applied, then allowed to dry. When it seemed thick enough to withstand careful handling, but still flexible enough to be bent in places, he removed the whole assembly from the figure. The Plasticine was scraped away from under the thin plastic skin, the edges trimmed and shaped, the ends which pass round the neck softened with cement and bent into place—*et voilà!* An airborne cloak, to genuine scale! The variations on this sort of theme are endless. Helmets, for instance; the basic cone can be modified in a number of attractive ways. With a rounder skull, card cheek-pieces, and central spine, it becomes a Viking or Saxon chieftain's helmet, in the style of the Sutton Hoo funerary treasure. Modern steel helmets nearly all evolved from some medieval shape; the British tin hat has a clear line of descent from the 'kettle hat' of the 13th Century man-at-arms, and with a bit of help from the files and some card strapping it could revert to type. The German coal-scuttle also traces its ancestry to the Middle Ages, and can be carved and filed into a pleasing sallet. Once the surface of a crudely-creased bulky torso and frocked legs have been produced by carving commercial kits about, a mail effect can be achieved by the patient modeller who rotates the tip of a fine rat-tail file against the surface of the plastic to make a series of tiny dips in a chain-mesh pattern. Swords, daggers, axes and maces can all be made from parts of more modern weapons with carved-sprue details. If a Pyrogravure can detail the surface of a sheepskin shabraque, it can do the same for a fur cloak. Afrika Korps trousered legs, with cross-gartering below the knee and boots shaved down to leather slippers, become in a short time the lower half of an earlier German warrior, perhaps one who fought Varus in the Teutoburger Forest . . . Think laterally, keep your spares box stocked, never miss a chance to add to your reference files—and enjoy yourselves!